TANKART

by Michael Rinaldi

rinaldistudiopress

A GUIDE TO PAINTING AND WEATHERING

WWII GERMAN ARMOR

contact information:
tankart@me.com

TANKART Vol. 1 WWII German Armor
Copyright © 2012 by Rinaldi Studio Press, LLC
All rights reserved.

All models, photography and text in this book are copyright © 2012 by the authors unless otherwise noted.

No part of this publication may be reproduced, stored in a retrieval system, or transmitted in any form, or by any electronic, mechanical, photocopying, recording, or otherwise, without the prior written permission of the publisher, Rinaldi Studio Press, LLC.

Graphic design, art direction and copy editing by Michael Rinaldi.

Author: Michael C. Rinaldi

Contributors: Mario Eens
                 Marijn van Gils

Published by:

Rinaldi Studio Press, LLC
9501 W Sahara Ave Unit 2272
Las Vegas, NV 89117

www.rinaldistudiopress.com
tankart@me.com

Designed in the USA
Printed in the USA
1st Edition, December 2012

US ISBN: 978-0-9883363-1-5

Special thanks to Rhodes Williams, Mario Eens, Marijn van Gils, and especially to my parents, without your neverending support none of this would have ever been possible.

To all of my model building friends and supporters, this book is for you.

FOREWORD

Is modeling art? A question some would answer with yes, and others with no. What exactly is art? Why is one painting regarded as a valuable piece of art and another as a piece of kitsch? As art is a sociological, psychological and historical bound understanding, there can be no exact definition to what art really is. In an attempt to give a definition one could argue that art is anything that is made by man with the aim to stimulate both the human senses and spirit by originality and/or beauty. If we now subject modeling to this definition, could we then say that some of it could be regarded as art…?

The same as with conventional pieces of art like paintings and sculptures there can be, should be, thought behind the creation of a model. Good models are not made without properly considering all aspects involved. Be it the camouflage pattern, adding damage, weathering and chipping, etc. Same as with 'proper' works of art, there needs to be a good composition behind it to attract the viewer's attention and above all to keep it. If the model does not look appealing, the viewer will get bored easily and wander off. So if not art modeling, good modeling could at least be regarded as artistic.

Mike Rinaldi, the author of the book you are about to enjoy, is a very artistic modeler. Like all good modelers, Mike has his own style that is yet very familiar and realistic. Every model he approaches in an artistic way, which results in models that keep the viewer interested and fascinated.

As in traditional art painters are inspired by each other's work, so are we modelers. It's fun to get ideas and techniques from fellow modelers and friends and in turn to inspire them. This way we should all become better modelers in the end. I for one have been inspired by Mike's work on many occasions and I'm sure by reading this book so will you…

Mario Eens

INTRODUCTION

The seed was planted for this book years ago. I have long desired to collate my models into a how-to book series, designed to educate and illustrate the latest in painting and weathering processes and ideas. But that wasn't the total emphasis behind this endeavor. I wanted the models to be something more, more than a magazine article, more than an online photo album. To me, the volume of work that I have created over the past 9 years has so much substance behind it, and in each case I have never been able to tell the full story of what went into them. Not just the *how*, but the *why* as well. The amount of editing for both the copy, and the number of images was often quite dramatic within each magazine article. I wanted to tell a more involved story; those personal details that I never have enough room to divulge when writing an article, or even a forum post. Those techniques that I am doing on a more subconscious level (that come from years of training and practice) to capture the mood, era, theater and climate that I visualize within each piece. To put it all together in an effort to share this knowledge with the hobby. It's been a driving force for a long time.

There has been a lack of fullfillment that I couldn't shake with the usual media outlets, and creating this book series was the ultimate expression of this goal. Even more so than producing DVDs, because you can't always refer to a DVD when needed, not everyone has their computer by their bench, finding the right "page" can be tedious, plus the very real copyright internet issues (piracy) that continues today, whereas a book can be easily handled, referred to quickly, studied intently, kept handy on the bench or desk, and so forth.

But what would set this book series apart from those that have preceeded it, or come after? To answer this question, I have to be frank and honest. First, I have had this continual thought that translating thoughts and actions into words and pictures should be accompanied by a certain level of candor. I wanted to stand back and look over your shoulder to provide a more authentic behind-the-scenes approach to the *how* and the *why* of each project, or technique. And from a more personal level of saying to the world, "This is who I am, and what I have created to share, teach and inspire." -- to give something back to a hobby.

Second, I think the usual publishing mediums are simply too restrictive by agenda, formats, or inclusive of other material. You see as a long time magazine writer, graphic designer, editor even, I have been involved with all aspects of magazine production and they are ultimately a major compromise to the true level of effort associated with professional model building. I don't mean that statement as overtly negative, or to insult their purpose, just that I feel a book can be so much more; a book can have a very different set of goals and reasons for being, and this does not have to follow the path of many newsstand publications. I could start with my own fresh outline. A book can be more from a graphics standpoint too, it can bring to bear a wonderful level of illustrative ability that is not restricted by a magazine's inherent format. Here is where I felt I could bring a lot to the table with my background as a professional designer, adding something more beyond the models themselves.

Third, and this is one of those more spiritual statements that we sometimes make, but I want my work to inspire. I recognize their is some ego in that statement, but that doesn't change the truth of it. Nothing drives me more on a personal modeling level than being inspired by someone else who has created a wonderful bit of work. I want to reciprocate that emotion and return the favor to so many of you out there that inspire me. It, to me, is one of those magical feelings we get from this hobby, you know when you flip thru an article, or see a model on the show stand, it just hits you. "Wow, that model is so amazing!" or, "Wow! how on earth did he do that!?" Honestly, it's that type of feeling that has sustained my drive to continue producing new models. It's a special thing we all share, and I feel strongly this book can really participate for each of us on that level.

Well, with all of that said, there is still the main crux of any such project -- compromise. As much as I would like to make a huge unlimited page count volume, that simply is not realistic from any level. Thus, I must reduce the work into a manageable and reproducable format. This initial volume on WWII German Armor, is what I would call the first snapshot at the massive variety of subjects available to chose from in this arena. My chapter choices are intended to cover most of the major camouflage finishes used, and hit on each key area of the painting and weathering process to give you maximum information over the length of this series. And then on top of that, I will speak specifically to certain techniques that pertain to nearly all projects, so you get a very complete picture of the methodologies at play.

I say this because inside these pages you will be given what I feel is a rare glimpse into a modeler's mindset, I will make every effort to put into words and pictures the techniques of using certain products and tools, and how I achieve the results that I do. Something that I hope is quite removed from the simple step-by-step process. I want you to know what's in my mind as I am working the process. Here is where this book will come to life and I believe you, the reader, will be drawn further in and find new methods, ideas, and inspiration to apply to your own work.

INTRODUCTION

What's in the book's name? I want to touch on this for just a moment to expand on my thoughts for the title of the series -- **TANK**ART. I have to believe the main reason you are reading this book is that the finishes I achieve have really drawn you to my work. I am known for my painting and weathering, and I'm rightly proud of this, but I didn't want to lay out a product that was not authentic to me, or to what I do. Honestly, I know I do not make the most historically accurate models, it's not my primary motivation for my work, nor is it for this book. Thus, the bulk of the focus will center around the notion of painting and weathering a tank model, pure and simple. All of which is fine with me, and all the while very honest to the type of modeler that I have become. And indeed our hobby is thankfully full of material that cover in wonderful detail all of the other aspects of the model building process, which also helps to free me from that responsibility and concentrate on what I do best.

TANKART is intended from the outset to compliment the currently available products on the market. The work inside is simply a representation of what can be achieved using similar methods and approaches to each project. The adage that what makes this hobby great is that there is no preset notions of what can or cannot be done is one I believe in, and my books are just one point of view towards that end.

MY MODELING PHILOSOPHY
I can imagine for a great many of you that there is a set of values, or guides, by which you govern your own work. I can also imagine that it is not a simple and easy set of parameters to come by; here is where experience must have an influence, and it was no different for me. It's taken me a long time, and a great many models, to realize certain aspects of what I do and how that dictates the final results of each piece. As I can only speak of myself about what my philosophies are, I must say it has become quite clear in recent works. For me, I can simplify and narrow it down to what I term -- *"artistic scale-ism"*. I don't think of myself as a hyper realist, as I have been called sometimes. Or a rivet counter, or any other number of terms we label us within the hobby. My focus, my driving mantra that pushes me, that keeps the work linear and always moving forward is the singular goal to recreate each area *in-scale* as I can muster, and within my defining artistic abilities.

There is a fine line between this idea and realism. To me, realism also speaks to historical accuracy, and here is where I usually diverge from the actual truth of a subject. Why? It's very simple really. You see unless there is a substantial number of photos of a specific vehicle at that moment in combat that has captured most aspects of its finish, how can you be too realistic in every area of the model? It becomes such a force to deal with that I lose that battle every time. I'm talking down to the tiniest chip or scratch. I usually only have the luxury of just one or two photos, and sometimes they are not even of the same vehicle. Achieving 100% realism has such a way of sapping my energy, I have come to realize this notion and embrace it. I think this could be described as semantics, but I feel it is a very viable point. In the end, I use photos as a guide, and usually nothing more. But again, everyone is different, and has very different goals within your own work.

I have other ideas that play an equally important role in this book and how best you can use it. In addition to the above main motto, part of my thesis is, quite strongly, that many techniques have a very broad range of "opacities" built within them, which nearly any modeler can apply to their work in as strong, or as subtle, of intensity as you desire, or require. To me, this is a very powerful concept that really expanded my viewpoint on the hobby, and how best to approach it. Suddenly, I went from having a lot of specific techniques and products for each specific need on each specific area of a model, to having far fewer processes, but each having a much broader level of application, thus greatly simplifying my step-by-step methods all around. This was a very freeing idea that has a huge influence on the outcome of each model, the timeframe required, the level of practice needed for each technique, and so forth. It changed how I approached a new piece, and my confidence grew at the same time.

As I set forth to proceed with this new series of modeling books, please take with it my gratitude for your continued support of what it is that I do. Like so many large projects, the level of committment and time required to see this become a reality requires so many thanks to all of the people touched by this process along the way. It simply would not have been possible otherwise. With that all said, please sit down at your workbench, put the overhead light on and turn the pages. I hope you will find within them the many ideas, techniques, methods, reasons why and how that I use to make my models, and from there begin your own journey within this wonderful hobby of ours. Enjoy the music in the background, smile at the cool subject before you, and always strive to push yourself further.

Like I say, "You can never have too small of a chip."

Best,

Michael C. Rinaldi

October 2012, Las Vegas, Nevada, USA

The subject of products and materials is always a bit controversial. So many of us have different ideas on what works and how much to spend; this greatly affects what is available for each of us on our workbenches. However, I can say towards that end is that I use what works for me, and has been proven over the course of nearly 70 models in the past few years. Having the confidence that what I am about to attempt with what product and knowing within spitting distance either way how it will turn out is very important. Approaching a model that you've just spent countless hours assembling, most likely adding considerable costs thru aftermarket accessories too, only to muff it in the paintbooth is never a pleasant episode. Believe me, we've all experienced that sort of crisis, so hopefully with some basic principles and solid choices, I can help you at least take a worthy crack at it.

OK, I am going to assume your model is built since that makes this conversation a lot easier to discuss. What tools you use to build a model is actually relatively similar across the planet; hobby knife, glue, sanding paper or sticks, putty, etc., with only the name brand and some minor differences coming into play. But with finishes, it is a whole different ballgame largely because it is a chemically based system of products.

○ Let me start by saying, the advice within this book is simply that, *advice*. It is not to be taken as gospel, or as this *must* be the way you do things. It is as simple as this is my way, and if you'd like to give it a shot, you will have a very good chance at success following with the information given.

PRIMER
I don't say to everyone that you must primer your model, but I do recommend it. I always prime with my work. Why? Because it has never let me down, the extra cost and insurance is rather minimal, and I have never had a paintjob fail *because* I primed a model. And while not always the case, usually my models are multi-media affairs, so the primer's main advantage here is to give the paint a common surface across the board, meaning the paint will adhere strongly, and the color will appear evenly as intended.

This process falls under the "keep it simple, stupid" mantra, and I tend to stick with what works over time with steps like these. If you are familiar at all with my work, you can easily guess my product of choice here -- Gunze Sanyo Mr. Surfacer 1200 in the aerosol can. I'm usually able to prime 3-4 models per can, so at approx. $10 each, that is fairly economical, and most importantly, the resulting finish is superb. Perfect for the paint, nearly any brand at that, to adhere to with strength, which is very important in the weathering stages. So yes, I do recommend that you prime. There are other quality products available from Tamiya, Testors, Vallejo and so on, and due to my dominant use of acrylic paints, Mr. Surfacer 1200 is my preferred product. Modern acrylic paint performs at a very high level in conjunction with it, thus it gets my vote.

PAINT
In truth, I only use acrylics. It is on the very rare occasion (just one time) that I have ventured into enamels (Humbrols), and for a good reason. I paint 100% indoors, and have never had the luxury of a properly built-in and vented spray booth, so I gravitated towards acrylics from a very early stage. That is not a bad thing though, because there

○ Gunze Sanyo Mr. Surfacer 1200 primer

○ **tips for achieving quality primed models:**

• make sure the surface is clean, free from dust, finger oils, glue stains, and all seams are filled and sanded properly. If need be, warm soapy water is usually adequate, dry thoroughly prior to spraying the primer.

• when using aerosols, spray outdoors if possible. The primer comes out fast, so move the can quickly from at least 10-12" away from the surface.

• most importantly, spray in light, thin coats. Let dry in between and ensure all visible areas are covered. 2 thin coats usually provides adequate coverage.

• it helps to use an old cardboard box, or small turntable to facilitate spraying the model upon, something to spin it with, or walk around easily. Primer sticks to skin quite well, so plan to use latex gloves if needed.

• an easy way to speed up drying time is to use a hairdryer on low heat. The model should be dry to the touch, with no primer residue remaining. Testing underneath is a good place to check.

are exceptional choices readily available to us from nearly any quality source.

Tamiya - these have been my personal favorite ever since I bought my first model in the local hobby store decades ago. While the color choices have not changed much since Godzilla first detroyed Toyko, a modern revelation has put these old school paints back on the map. Tamiya's (and Gunze's Aqueous colors too) are chemically quite similar to a lacquer in their properties, and appropriately called *acrylic lacquers*. I'm no expert, but this tidbit of knowledge was passed around a few years ago that said if you thin them with Tamiya's own lacquer thinner they will airbrush with the best paints around, including enamels. OK, so that sort of flies in the face of my efforts to spray indoors, but hey I can't win them all. After some tests, I was happy to realize that this is indeed very true and I found the ability to achieve smooth finishes and extremely tight camo patterns an experience I have not had the pleasure of before when using acrylics. It was like a whole new lease on life. I have maintained drawers of Tamiya paints in my storage cases, but they were rarely used until combined with said lacquer thinner, now I use them quite often. (And try to use Tamiya, Gunze, or Gaianotes brand lacquer thinners, or a high quality art store brand -- trust me on this point).

Lifecolor - these acrylics hail from Italy and are one of the newest brand on the market, and what an array of color choices. They have recently expanded into pre-packaged color packs that focus on specific themes or subjects, and overall they are a superb brand of paint. For two reasons; first, they airbrush thinned with simple tap water, and are nearly odorless, thus well suited for indoor painting. Second, they brush paint with the best of them and this gives them incredible versatility, again thinned with water. Some guys have experienced difficulty making a transition to them from regular enamel painting, but once the thinning ratios are properly sorted, they perform at the highest levels. They have excellent leveling qualities and this is important when the paint dries tightly around fine details. They also dry dead matte and this gives us maximum options to impart mettalic sheens from there, versus having to flatten them further. Their increasing popularity means they are readily available from a lot of good online sources. And I will give one additional recommedation, I find Lifecolor some of the best out-of-the-bottle colors available, and they look right to my "eye", or usually *in-scale*, something critical for success.

Vallejo - these are also exceptional paints and arrive via Spain. They have been on the market for a few years now and produce a dizzying array of products, beyond paint pro-

○ Tamiya Acrylics {Japan}

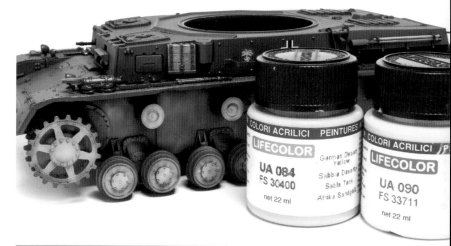

○ Lifecolor Acrylics {Italy}

○ Vallejo Model Air Acrylics {Spain}

ducts even. For our purposes, the **Model Air** and **Model Color** lines are the two most important. Model Color is engineered for brush painting, so figure modelers are well versed in their quality, but this also translates to painting details on armor. In addition, they are sold in bottles with a convenient eye-dropper style top, and this makes for very efficient usage overall. My only real gripe with Vallejos, (and most acrylics in general), is that they dry rapidly on the tip of the airbrush, with the resulting paint build-up requiring constant attention to keep the airbrush performing perfectly. Vallejos are the worst culprit with this, so I tend to shy away from them in hotter drier weather, or add a lubricant to stem the drying. Beyond that, they are excellent paints and considered one of the best for our hobby needs. Also they are readily available from almost all popular online and local hobby shops. Overall Vallejos have great color choices, spray and brush paint very well, and dry quickly to a durable surface allowing us to proceed quickly to the weathering stages.

A couple of quick points on Lifecolor and Vallejo. They are chemically different from Tamiya, thus they are not interchangeable. Well, I certainly do not recommend mixing either brand with Tamiya; I have not had any success in doing so. I tend to keep to one brand of paint throughout the course of the model's paintjob, so the decision on which to use, and when, usually comes down to the chosen scheme and what color choices I have at hand. And I must say, it is not a popularity contest for me, they all work great after some practice; they are a tool just like any other, and combined with a quality airbrush all of them will offer the required needs of each project.

As for other brands of paint, I cannot comment with much authority because the 3 brands above are my primary choices. Space is rather tight at the end of the day, and with paint in general, I find practice and experience are as vital (or more so) than the label on the bottles.

AIRBRUSH & COMPRESSOR

I have to tackle this devisive topic because what airbrush to use is akin to trying to advice the public on what brand of car to drive--heated arguments and debates are rather neverending. But, be that as it may, and because airbrushes and compressors are regarded as one of the primary (and the most expensive) tools you will be required to purchase, it is a must that I discuss these two items to some degree.

In my experience, I have had great luck with my chosen airbrushes, and over the past few years have acquired certain tastes on what features I prefer. I look for these features regardless of brand, so I will stick with my advice on them rather than the brand names. These ideas would most definitely come from experience and usage over time, since the painting of a lot of models will illuminate quite a few things, undoubtedly.

Starting with the airbrush, if you can only afford one, then by all means save up and purchase the absolute best one you can afford. Price point is a great indicator and while cheap overseas eBay airbrushes look tempting, I would say be ready to spend at least $80-100 depending on the brand. Again, I am purposely shying away from saying you should use this brand or that, but on my bench I have the Tamiya Super Fine, and the larger of the two MiG Productions airbrushes, which is a great entry level hobby airbrush. I would also imagine many of you already have your setups, so from there I can only emphasis practice, practice, and more practice. It does make a world of difference. Once you learn to thin the paint correctly and set your pressures, it can be a beautiful thing when the paint flows as it should.

I do have some specific feature preferences, and while few, they are critical to how I spray and achieve my finishes. The first feature I prefer, is the top trigger style airbrush. I like how I can control the air flow in this manner, and not that the gun-trigger style is better or worse, this is simply my preference. Second, I like the top feed cup style because they are easier to clean. Yes, the side or bottom feeds means you can switch colors easier, however, I always clean in between colors, so quick, easy cleaning takes precedent for me. Third, and most important, I always add an adjustable rear handle that controls how far back the trigger (and thus the needle) can be pulled back. This feature is critical for spraying camo schemes, and when used in conjunction with the right thinning ratio and air pressure allow for maximum paint control on tight or very faint camo patterns. I cannot tell you how much this feature has allowed me to be accurate in this regards, so each of my brushes has one fitted. Some higher priced AB already come so equipped, but if not, definitely order one immediately!

Beyond that, I can add that I maintain an airbrush for each chemical type of paint that I use. Thus, I have one for spraying Tamiya and other lacquer based products, one for the Lifecolor and Vallejo products. Why? Well it goes back to the cleaning topic again. I found over the years, trying to use one airbrush for all paints takes it toll on the internals, and often when an airbrush stopped performing properly this was the main reason. Some other type of paint was still lodged inside, and the new paint was causing havoc with the needle in most cases, in essence small dried gunk of different paints would build up inside. Once I switched to dedicated airbrushes for each paint type used, life got a lot easier. This is obviously a lot more critical if you paint a lot, like I do. (In a normal year, I am painting 10-12 models.) Which is another reason I prefer the top feeds, they are simpler to disassemble, and the least amount of time spent doing so is fine with me.

In regards to the compressor, in a perfect world, every modeler would use a similar setup to mine. Once obtained, I never looked back. In fact, my Iwata airtank-style compressor has performed flawlessly for over 6 years now, (mine is the 3.5 liter capacity Power Jet), and what it does is two very wonderful things. One, with its large internal capacity air-tank it builds up air pressure that is then readily available for immediate use, silently, which leads to a far quieter painting experience. If not familiar, these airtank compressors turn on automatically once the air pressure is below the setting, and refilling the tank takes about 30 seconds. While it does kick on and off with some noise and vibration, it is a far more pleasant process than using a straight blower compressor that is running continuously. It's one of those things where once you experience it, you can't believe you ever used the other ones.

And two - my compressor can also run two separate airbrushes, which can be very handy for camo painting. Now, I know this is strictly a cost-based issue, but I strongly recommend the same or a similar airtank compressor, and like I said, it has performed without a hiccup and will provide many years of professional level use.

With all that said, however, there are other great options on the market today. I believe both Badger and Iwata produce small relatively quiet pump-style compressors that modernize the experience to where the neighbors won't be knocking on your door at 2AM asking you to stop.

As to air pressures and thinning ratios, I believe they are related to your region and time of year (how your work area is heated and cooled), or put another way -- the environment. While I will definitely tell you what I do on each project, remember that I spend my time indoors in Southern California and Nevada, which are essentially arid dry desert climates with relatively low humidity values. And in the cases where I did live next to the ocean, my painting did perform differenty to living inland, so I had to make adjustments. What works for me in April in SoCal, maybe an entirely different matter to a modeler in Canada in November, or another guy in Northern Europe in August. I think it is one of those dark topics we rarely discuss and honestly, it is as much art as it is science.

Advice is usually only a starting point, and fine tuning the ratios to your needs and region will be necessary. In simple terms, the two important areas of viscosity and drying time are the most critical properties with airbrushing. So that means your chosen air pressure and thinning ratio will be affected by your environment, how you are laying it on the model, the camo scheme, and so on. There are lots of variables involved, and the main reason I think the common questions of "How much do you thin brand X?", or "What is your compressor setting?" are not simple de-facto answers for everyone. Otherwise, it would be a slamdunk topic and the answers placed in the pinned FAQ threads on all the online forums.

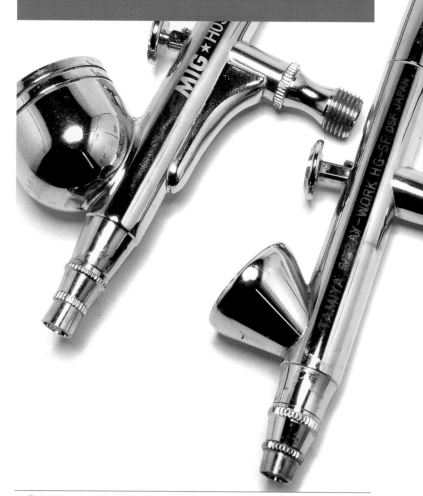

tips for achieving quality airbrush thinning ratios and air pressure settings:

• in a very general, and simplistic formula, here is a good starting point:

for the thinning, I start with a 50-50 thinner-to-paint ratio, and from there I add either more paint or thinner depending on my need for a basecoat or a camo pattern.

my compressor is typically set around 12-15psi for general basecoat painting. For tighter camo requirements, I will up the ratio of thinner-to-paint, and drop the psi. This is only a simple guide, but a very good one, and should get you in the race right out of the gate, especially if this topic is a source of frustration, or you are new to airbrushing.

PRO-TIP: always, always, always spray in light thin coats and build up the color gradually. You do this to maintain the molded detail as crisply as possible. Heavy thick coats of paint will ruin the model's details. The paint also dries much faster and evenly, all desired properties.

○ Tamiya's Super-Fine (HG-SF) airbrush, next to MIG Production's large cup airbrush.

FILTERS AND WASHES

I will discuss the attributes of applying both filters and washes in much greater detail in the subsequent project chapters, so the use and purpose of each one will only be touched upon now to help set the background. In a tried and proven fashion, I paint with acrylic basecoats and then use oil and enamel-based washes and filters on top of them because of the durability factor in how acrylics are not chemically destroyed in the process. This creates a very stable and repeatedable basic painting outline whereby any modeler can achieve success on every occassion. Considering the rising costs of everything we buy, this is important to our long term mental and fiscal health.

Let me first add some definitions, because these two are the most commonly confused and misrepresented as to what they are, and how best to use them.

Filters - In essence, a *filter* is a tinting layer. For traditional painters this is referred to as a *glaze coat*. The intent is to alter the underlying color in a very subtle manner, adding visual depth to the affected area. A filter can be applied to a small area, or as an overall layer to the entire model in a harmonizing effect. It is created by taking 95% thinner to about 5% paint and can be applied by brush or via an airbrush. When I make my own, I prefer to use Humbrol paint, which give consistent results.

And, as you are likely aware of, today we also have ready-made filters from both **MiG Productions** and **AK Interactive** that facilitate this process, and both do the job equally well. And for those of you that do not use enamels, Vallejo now provides acrylic filters too, but in each case it is important to keep in mind its purpose--filters are for tinting base colors. I like to think of them like a colored filter on a camera lens, they add another color layer of depth to the equation.

Washes - These differ from filters in two distinct areas. One, they are created from a much more concentrated ratio, anywhere from 10-20% paint-to-thinner. Two, they are intended to enhance details by providing additional false shadow-like qualities, visually forcing the raised, or engraved, details to pop out more. Traditionally, wash colors are typically dark browns and black colors, but depending on the model or theater of action, light tones to represnt dust and sand are also used to good effect.

Again, washes and filters are easily made at home with enamel or oils, or you can use the ready-made products from **MIG Prod.**, **AK Interactive,** or **Vallejo**. I try not to overthink the washes though, keep the premise simple and straight forward.

○ Sin Industries Filter MiG Productions {Spain}

○ Pinwash created from Humbrol enamels {UK}

tips when using filters and pinwashes:

• overall filters are easily applied via an airbrush. The results are very controllable in this manner, let dry in between each coat to decide if another layer is necessary.

• I always apply a pinwash with a #2 round quality brush. This brush holds a good quantity in the bristles and the fine tip allows for precision applications, important for a pinwash.

• filters and pinwashes are initial weathering stages, it's best to make them subtle, using the susequent weathering steps to strengthen and enhance certain areas.

PIGMENTS

Arguably, pigments are some of my favorite (and most important) weathering products to use. They are simply one of the best mediums to represent dust, dirt and mud, even better than what you can find in your garden, in my opinion, due to their excellent in-scale and adhesion qualities. Because of the chemical nature of what painting and weathering is all about, pigments fit into this scheme perfectly, and there are methods and addtional products that provide a cohesive bond between this process and the other weathering stages, both visually and physically.

From my extensive pigment experience, I have come to rely heavily on the pigments MiG Production. They really do an outstanding job with them, they have a great range of colors, prices are reasonable, and they are readily available in today's market. Even my local hobby shop stocks them, which says a lot, and when used properly they last a very long time over the course of many models. They work as intended and provide some outstanding results. Recently AK Interactive is also selling pigments, but they are usually included in their pre-packaged weathering sets along with other washes and filters, and they work exactly the same as MP pigments.

Pigments are concentrated ground-up paint pigments, and these are simply superior in adhesion and color saturation to pastels, which were commonly used before pigments came along. The idea is essentially the same -- to represent earth effects on a vehicle, however pigments allow for the entire range of dust to wet mud, and everything in between. They can be applied dry, with a "fixer" agent added, or pre-mixed into various solutions and applied wet to the surface of the model. My main preference is the former, I almost always apply them dry to a model, then add the appropriate fixer to set them into place. Once dry, they create some of the most realistic earthen effects possible.

○ My pre-mixed pigment colors, plus brush that I use to apply them to the model.

○ **tips for achieving success with pigments:**

• applying pigments over a matte surface is best for adhesion, so try to keep the lower hull area free from any gloss varnishes. Pigments will cover early pinwashes and filters, so be prepared to repeat some of those steps after the pigments are applied for best results.

• mixing pigments together into pre-mixed batches creates vastly improved visual characteristics when dry. Just like real dirt & mud, there are many colors in each area of earth, so using the same idea with pigments will add a lot of depth to this area on the model.

• pigments can be mixed just as easily as paints. Use old 35mm film canisters to store these mixed pigments. I like to make a *light*, *medium*, and *dark* mixture for each project.

• layering pigments from light to dark is an excellent way to add realism and visual depth. Apply the layers logically from top-to-bottom, and from light-to-dark for best results. Random effects are always preferred, so do not try to be too precise.

○ Pigments can be used for both earth effects and for snow effects.

15

DEFINING WEATHERING

To properly discuss armor weathering, it helps to define the topic. To me, weathering means the affects on the surface of a tank from combat, climate, theater of operation, crew usage, time in service, intensity of the era, and mother nature. I look at weathering as the combination of the vehicles *patina* from its use, plus the affects of the *natural setting* of the subject. In the wristwatch world, the Japanese have a term for this idea called *wabi,* which loosely translates to "the beauty of an object over the course of it's lifetime". I find this idea very applicable to armor modeling. It's one of those subjects where the final look is strongly dictated by these principles, and to me this has a very artistic implication, hence the book's title -- **TANK**ART.

We should also include the maintenance of the subject and the ability of the crew/owner to repair the vehicle at any given time. Certain subjects, such as those covered

in the German armor volumes will have a clear indication of this as a result of their struggling efforts to keep their vehicles operational under constant combat situations. All of these are factors in how a subject can be portayed, and this allows for a ton of variations for us to pursue and illustrate.

With that general outline of what weathering entails, the next integral idea of this book series is how best to represent the myriad of effects possible. And it can be a staggering endeavor. Paint wear and tear, dust, dirt, mud, oil stains, rust streaks, paint chips and scratches, tracks, barrels, so on and so on. All require a certain level of attention, and the best method that I have found to tackle these is to *layer* the effects throughout the course of the project.

LAYERING

Layering is at the heart of everything that I do. It is the fundamental cornerstone of my work, nothing gets past this idea. I layer all of my processes, one over the other, and repeat as often as I feel is necessary to achieve the final results. One thing I learned is that rarely does an effect achieve the desired result in just one go, or one application. The models you see in these pages are the results of a constant process of layering one technique (or process) upon another, and not being limited to a strict outline for the order of them, I only use a simple guideline that directs this flow.

This *layering* concept, which I have mentioned since my earliest articles, is driven by the subject and theater of operation of the vehicle. Naturally, a winter schemed project will take on different characteristics to a desert themed project. So it helps to have an understanding of each technique and how it's best applied to a specific stage of the project. When to add a pinwash? When to go over a filtered area with another filter? Where to add paint chips? These questions, and many more, become both routine and endless. Each model brings its own set of values to them and this is where experience and practice come into focus.

The beauty of the *layering* concept is that it requires fewer actual techniques to implement. With a refined concept of what techniques provide superior results for a given effect, we can narrow down our processes allowing us to gain both quicker expertise with them, and greater efficiency over the course of a project. This is very important because it allows for the flow of a project to be better maintained, and this is a huge consideration for so many of us, myself included. I can't count how many times

○ This model of a StuG III Ausf. B in winter whitewash can be seen in Canfora Publishing's StuG book.

momentum has dithered away on a project, causing delays for a project under a deadline, whether for print, or for a show. While not critical for every model, having a nice flow to the work does keep a project going and this adds a lot of satisfaction element to the hobby. It is probably fair to say, the so called shelf-queens frustrate the bulk of us. I know it does for me. I love it when a model is completed, and this has been an underlying theme to my work and how I develop ideas and concepts to that end. Greater modeling efficiency is at the heart of why I developed the *Oil Paint Rendering* process, in fact.

ARTISTIC SCALE-ISM

I know this is a made up word, but in fact it properly describes the other basic driving concept behind my work. To achieve a desired effect *in-scale* is my primary focus behind each process and technique that I use -- it's the very foundation of what I am trying to achieve. For me, this supercedes such diversive topics as "do tanks get paint chips?" or "you are using mud to cover construction flaws", comments to me that become fundamentally irrelevant in the face of what is *in-scale*, or not. The challenge of creating these effects *in-scale* are where we need to focus our efforts instead. How can a certain effect be properly rendered to be both believable

WEATHERING PRINCIPLES

and *in-scale*? This is where I drive my car to work every morning. This is my job, in essence. If I can achieve these concepts, then I feel good that I am doing my job correctly. This is what dictates what techniques, products, tools, and methods I use to arrive at the final conclusion of a project.

I have a saying, one I'm rather fond of using: "*You can never have too small of a chip.*" I say this because, one, I feel it is true, and two, I think it keeps myself in check; pushes me to achieve greater levels of both realism and artistic technique. Becoming stagnant in one's work is the quickest way to death in my eyes. Part of my core training was to continually seek a path for steady and manageable improvements. In my design education, I was taught to never fall in love with my work, in fact disposing of old work is preferable (saving a record of it, of course), and in our hobby world I find this principle very applicable and allows for the necessary growth factor to be achieved that pushes us to create objects to the level seen on these pages. For some of you, this will likely be a foreign concept. But it was the key factor

○ 1/35 Bison I illustrating a Panzergrau paint scheme in the French campaign during the summer of 1940

○ 1/72 Panzer IV Ausf. F1 in winter whitewash over Panzergrau in the Russian front.

○ 1/35 Befehls Panther Ausf. G in a whitewash over a Dunkelgelb base coat in late 1945 on the Eastern Front.

in having each model stand on its own merits, while still being a viable project within my library of models. It is this greater body of work that has allowed me to create this new book series. Without it, I couldn't expand upon these principles and illustrate them fully.

That constant goal *to never have too small of a chip*, is part of this process, and it works well with the *layering* concept within my overriding principle of *artistic scale-ism*. How all of this is brought together within each model project is the root of the book's model chapters, and with that said, I feel strongly, you the reader, will be able to discern and embrace these ideas for your own work.

So how is all of this acheived? I like to break it down into the basic elements for discussion. It starts with the model ready for painting, and the particular color scheme and unit markings decided upon. It is very desirable to have your reference images and/or color plates at hand, study them and plan out certain aspects of the wear and tear, and where you want to focus your weathering steps upon. Again, only you can determine this, but it is highly recommended to have a general idea in your head before setting out.

GENERIC PAINT & WEATHERING OUTLINE

Painting is the first stage to be completed. Quality paintjobs are the foundation for all that is to come, so time and practice are immeasurable factors, including the camo coats.

Chipping is going to depend on how you want the overall model to look, so you can use HS layers early on, or you can apply chips after the paintjob is complete via a sponge, or a brush (or all of the above if you prefer).

Markings follow next, and while there are tons of choices, I tend to paint them on whenever possible.

Filters are used to tie all the colors together, tone down certain areas and/or markings, to tint colors, and add depth to the general color scheme.

Pinwashes create false shadows to help bring out the detail in the model.

Oil Paints are used to render the surface affects out to their fullest affect.

Pigments add the dust, dirt and mud elements.

Heavy washes and stains are added to emphasis used areas like the engine deck and crew hatches.

HAIRSPRAY TECHNIQUE

In depth explanation of this powerful technique

HS TECHNIQUE - BACKGROUND

It is fair to say the hairspray technique has been a very influential process in my work since 2007. I was in attendance at the Euro Militaire show that year when Phil Stutcinkas won Best-in-Show with his impressive Panzer IV Ausf. J set in a winter scene in Hungary 1945. The paintjob of the tank itself was staggering, and his subsequent articles on how he achieved it forever changed my modeling world.

After the show, and working on my first hairspray model, I spoke with Phil at length about his ideas and how he came to use hairspray for this process. His primary goal was to illustrate, as realistically as possible, a heavily worn-off whitewash coat without damaging the model, and after trying a multitude of products discovered the power of hairspray and why it is so effective. First, it is water soluble and basically inert, (designed for human topical usage it won't harm a model's paintjob), and the removal process is very controllable in both quantity of the top coat to be removed, and how much effort is required to remove it, which is crucial for models with delicate photo-etch details attached. Many forms of recreating distressed paint can easily damage, or remove, PE parts and this is a prime concern with more involved projects.

It was in the course of this discussion, that I realized the true power of the technique. I quickly discerned that while it worked perfectly for whitewash finishes, it had the ability to be the ultimate paint chipping process as well. The shape, style, formation, whatever you want to call it, of the resulting chips and scratches are to my eyes spot on, and most importantly *in-scale*. This was a real "moment" for me, and I have not looked back ever since. I now use the HS technique in nearly every model's paintjob, usually from the very beginning to create layers of chips and scratches from the nearly impossible to see, all the way to same level of heavily distressed whitewash finishes. This chapter will go into depth about how to achieve success with this very powerful idea.

TRES TWO™
ultra fine mist

professional formula
HAIR SPRAY

NET WT 11 OZ (311 g)

HS FOR ALL CHIPPING

The real strength of using hairspray for chipping is that it allows us to recreate this effect in the most *in-scale* manner possible today. Add to this, the excellent randomness charecteristics and it becomes quite clear why using HS to perform all of the chipping tasks is the best method to use. I say this even with the quality of using the sponge method, which is arguably a bit easier, however I think the shape and formation of the chips and scratches, (which are just as important), from using HS has a far more realistic visual effect.

Implementing this idea into the paintjob from the very beginning was the key factor in pulling out the full value in the HS technique, especially with German armor finishes and red primer being such a prominent element throughout their wartime painting. By utilizing HS from the start, we can now layer the chipping effects in a very realistic manner and the resulting chips are actually true paint chips, they look and act just like real chips, as opposed to those painted on after the fact, which require even more efforts to make look real. HS eliminates a lot of that extra effort on the back end, and building the chips into the paintjob from the first step is both more efficient and provides superior results.

With that said, let me start with a basic breakdown of the process, and then I will talk specifically about which products perform the best and how best to achieve a variety of finishes depending on the type of paint job and theater of operation.

GENERAL HS OUTLINE

1) Red primer is the best starting point for a regular combat vehicle. For severe weathering such as a burned out tank, start with a dark metal layer first.

2) HS #1 apply two even coats of HS.

3) Base coat this will be either Panzergrau, or Dunkelgelb depending on the timeframe of the subject.

○ *Stage One* - red primer layer is covered in two even coats of HS. A hairdryer is used to quickly dry the first layer before applying the second. You can paint the top coat as soon as HS layer two is dry.

○ *Stage Two* - the appropriate base coat is applied next, in this case it's a light shade of dunkelgelb. Tamiya has proven to provide the best chipping results, and I typically thin it with water for easier chipping.

○ *Stage Three* - Wet one section at a time with enough water to see the glossy sheen, but no so much it pools on the surface, or drips off. Let it sit for a few seconds, up to a minute sometimes, and then begin to gently scrub the paint in the areas you want them. Work slowly, utilize motions that replicate the marks in a natural manner.

21

4) Chipping using water and brushes, the initial paint chips are created.

5) HS #2 this will be for either chipping the camo colors, or a whitewash coat depending on the scheme in question.

6) Chipping assuming it's for the camo colors, this will be a subtle effort, utilizing the same process as above. For a whitewash layer it will typically be a lot more extreme.

HS APPLICATION

With that general understanding of the process, let me turn my attention to the actual product itself. I'll start by saying it's an advantage to use an off-the-shelf HS product from the store. It is proven to work in a superior manner, and it does not require an extra airbrushing stage (and the resulting cleaning of it), so I would recommend a quality brand like Tresemme I show here. It should be a *fine-mist* aerosol style can, the spritzer style bottles do not lay down even layers and are too hard to control. I find the men's products have less perfume, but honestly they tend to have more pleasant odors than the rest of the chemicals we typically use.

Distance from the model, and the speed of your hand's spraying motion are also key factors. I

tips for success using the hairspray technique:

• like most techniques, moderation is best, even with extreme finishes. Work slowly in small sections, use lots of reference, even if not of the same vehicle.

• for smaller areas, HS can be decanted into an airbrush and then used for a specific spot, or for small tools and stowage items added later. It will keep a very long time decanted in a spare 35mm film canister.

• HS quantity matters. Also how it is sprayed onto the surface. Smooth even coats perform the best in a controllable fashion. Too much HS will cause large paint flakes to occur without warning, so better to have less HS overall if you are unsure. If you know you have too much on the model, simply rinse it off before applying the paint. Dry it off and try again.

• sometimes it requires us make a small hole in the paint surface to get the process, find a less obvious spot and make a small scratch with your knife.

• most importantly - practice, practice, and then practice again. And again. It helps more than anything else.

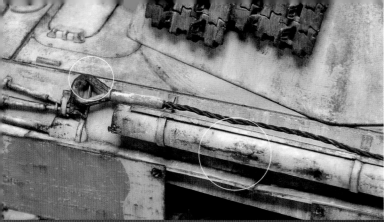

○ Panther in winter whitewash over dunkelgelb paintjob. A cumi-
lative project that includes HS for all the regular chips, and then
again for the distressed whitewash finish.

○ Ferdinand in a very opaque whitewash finish, over a two-tone Dunkelgelb and red brown camo scheme. There are three layers of HS
and whitewash present on this model for maximu depth.

○ Panzer IV in basically the same three HS layers of whitewash as
the Ferdinand, used to express maximum depth for a distressed
whitewash camo over a Panzergrau basecoat.

○ Sturm 33B illustrating a more straightforward and normal HS whitewash finish over a Panzergrau base coat. This is further enhanced
with mapping on top of the white to add even more interest.

○ Sd.Kfz 251/22 illustrating the extent to using HS from the first
layer of paint to the last, including a very faint whitewash effect.
HS was even used under the hand painted numbers.

○ Panzer IV in the desert for a more severe style of chips consistent
with that sort of hostile environment. The excess heat will cause
paint to crack more causing a larger areas with sharp chip edges.

23

○ Using HS for interior chipping is just as viable. The process is no different to the exterior, and on this Sd.Kfz 251/22 interior it started with red primer, HS layer, Dunkelgelb paint, and then the chipping.

○ For this Panzer IV DAK model, the interior visible through the open hatches gives an opportunity to chip and scratch the interior paint as well. It is simple, yet very effective, given how much can actually be seen.

troubleshooting HS chipping issues: ○

• most chipping problems start with the quantity of HS applied. When no chips are happening then too little HS was applied, and when large chipped flakes happen easily then too much HS was applied. Practice with two even coats.

• the thickness of the outer layer of paint is important as well. Too thick of paint will simply be unable to perform properly, with erratic chipping the result. Keep in mind where the chips will occur and spray less paint in those areas.

like to hold the model in my left hand (I'm naturally a right hander), at arm's length (at least 12-18" away), and with the HS can in my right hand, start spraying in front of the model, (before the HS hits the surface), and work across the model to the rear in one smooth quick motion, stopping *after* I pass the edge of the hull. This technique is exactly the same that is taught for any type of hand held aerosol spraying. The worst thing to do is to move slowly, and stop on the model itself. The volume of HS will simply pool too fast, and this is not what you want.

Work your way around the entire model in this manner. Lay down one even coat. It is best to cover all of it, rather than risk not having some where you need it. Once completed, let it dry to the touch, either by air or hairdryer. Then repeat the process for a second layer, and yes, once dry you can paint straight away.

PAINT APPLICATION

With the model ready for the second layer of color (the layer of paint that will be chipped), spray the base coat just as you would under normal circumstances. Looking at the Tiger II photos on page 22, you can clearly see the dunkelgelb is a solid layer of color. Other than thinning the Tamiya paints with water, I do nothing different than I normally would for spraying the base coat.

Why? That means the resulting chips will be a lot fewer, some hard to create even, and this is very intentional. When chipping a normal combat tank, we want some chips and scratches to give it life, but it's not the same effect as a heavily worn whitewash. By spraying the paint in a normal opaque manner, we can control the chips a lot more keeping them from overpowering the model. The goal is, as I mentioned before, for everything to be *in-scale*, and that means also the quantity, not just their size. My general rule for the size and quantity on a combat tank is to pull back 2-3' from the model and squint my eyes, if I can't see the chips and scratches it is just about right. They should just about disappear when you squint from a few feet away.

A quick note on thinning Tamiya paints with water for the HS process...typically I thin them with lacquer thinner, but in this instance the superior adhesion qualities make using an opaque base coat difficult to chip with water. It simply creates too strong of a barrier, so thinning them with water gives better results in conjunction with HS chipping.

CHIPPING - WATER, BRUSHES, ETC.

With the paint applied, it's now time for the fun part. I have a small cup of water handy, it is simple room temperature tap water, and a couple of chipping brushes. One has short

○ Using HS for nearly any form of chipping, including removing overspray on this red primer area of the model. It was easier than masking the surface off and blended in better with the rest of the paintjob due to its slight irregularities of the project.

○ HS is capable of achieving hard stark chips for an appearance typical for a veteran combatant or heavily worn out vehicle. Also note the large variety of sizes within the small confines of the surfaces that are chipped. This adds to the realism effect.

○ Using new chipping fluids in place of HS is a great method for smaller details and stowage items added after the vehicle's paintjob. It is useful to spray the parts separately and create the chipping effects individually, for some added visual variety.

and stiff bristles, the other a flat thin bristle brush, and another with an angled flat tip. This will cover most of the chipping needs, and then I have a couple of sharp toothpicks, and the ever handy Tamiya Paint Stir Stick, which is smooth chromed metal with excellent fine edges for making scratches with. Combined together these tools provide the best results for most style of marks required.

For the actual water application, brush a small section of the model with just enough water to get the paint wet (it should look wet, in fact), but not so much that it runs and drips off the model. Typically the water takes a few moments to work its way through and then you can begin to scrub the surface. It may take a little more time, or more water at times, but you can usually tell in most cases. The water is NOT dissolving the paint, it is dissolving the HS and taking whatever is on top of it with it. So what this means for an opaque top coat is that you typically need to start the process on a sharp edge to get the first chip going, and then you simply work your way around the model in a controlled manner.

I use the short bristle brush for most basic chipping, the flat brush for those areas I want to have some soft faded gradations (great for

○ **hairspray vs. chipping fluid:**

• at the time of writing there are now dedicated chipping fluid products on the market from **AK Interactive** and **MiG Productions** designed to replicate HS style of chipping. They are essentially repackaged hairspray in a non-aerosol bottle for use with your airbrush for its application. I've used them both and they work as intended, and will give satisfactory chipping results. However, there are some areas of note to be aware of:

• airbrushing two even layers of a clear liquid is a little tricky, it's tough to discern the actual quantity applied. I prefer a higher psi in fact, spraying faster from a farther distance than normal painting.

• the chipping was a little more sporadic, but that may be because it is different solution to my normal HS product. Test and practice beforehand.

• using an airbrush to apply does defeat some of the ease with which this technique was intended and the results aren't superior. I find using them for chipping smaller details like tools useful.

○ The motion of the brush is crucial to perform certain styles for the chips and scratches. Use a motion related to the type of action that was likely to create the wear in the top layer of paint.

Note: This StuG III Ausf. B can be seen within Canfora Publishing's book On Display Vol. 2 StuG III.

○ It is important to focus the removal of the top layer in a realistic fashion. Reference photos helps tremendously, but also common sense is used in areas where it is very difficult to reach and remove the paint.

tips for achieving succes with winter whitewash HS chipping: ○

• use Tamiya XF-2 White thinned with water. Spray the white in irregular patches, leaving the edges covered in less paint for superior chips and scratches.

• it is possible to layer the whitewash layers as much as desired. Three layers of whitewash can create a very deep and interesting aesthetic not achievable with any other method.

• combine whitewashes with the mapping technique, adding further areas of random opaque white patches. This will give the whitewash a very natural and appealing look.

whitewashes), and the sharp angled brush for longer chips and more linear style marks. The toothpick and Stir Stick are usually reserved for dedicated long scratches and require single one-direction swipes to achieve. But the marks are mostly dependent on the motion of your hand as much as the brush tip itself. It is not unlike drawing, the motion of the hand will dictate the marks of the pen, so it is with the chipping brushes. And variety is key and this is where practice and experience really help a lot. I have found when discussing with experienced modelers that it itakes them 2 to 3, sometimes as many as 5 or 6 projects under their belt using HS to realize the level of refinement possible. They all have that "ah-hah!" model where it clicked, so I cannot say this emphatically enough -- practice, practice, and then practice again. The process is quite simple and very straightforward, no need to overthink anything about it, it is as simple as described, but the subtleties are what take time and practice. And then more practice, but so it is with this hobby from basic airbrushing to figure painting, to HS, you must put in the time with it to achieve its best results.

PAINT BRANDS FOR HS CHIPPING

This is another topic that gets a bit diversive, I would guess mainly because we tend to use what we have at our bench at hand, or what is available to easily purchase. I've tried them all, even enamels, and, in general, all paint brands will work because, again, the water is dissolving the HS not the paint. It is simply a matter of allowing enough water through the top surface to make it happen. Here are what I feel the best paints to use for HS chipping:

Tamiya - in a perfect world, this conversation ends here. They simple do work the best for this technqiue because of their unqiue properties, or rather the lack of properties they have. Because Tamiya acrylic paint does not dry to a solid vinyl layer of a shell like the other two acrylics, the results are superior, easier to control and replicate. The main reason is the chips are finer in appearance and more realistic as a result. When used as I describe above, they rarely flake off in large undesired chunks of paint. I prefer Tamiya for both regular base coat paint and extreme finishes using whitewash or heavy desert paint wear.

Vallejo - these are, as we know, vinyl acrylics, and because of this charateristic are not going to perform to quite the same level as Tamiya. Yes, they do work and can have great chipping results, but it requires a few areas of thin color application to allow for the water to get under, and be prepared for the occasional large paint flake to happen. With Vallejo, they chemically harden after a period of time, and this is when it gets a lot more difficult to control or predict the style and size of the chip to be made.

Lifecolor - while these are very similar to Vallejo in make-up they perform somewhere in between Tamiya and Vallejo in how they can be affectively chipped. They dry like Vallejo but their shell characterisitics are not as pronounced as Vallejo's, so success is a little easier achieved. They also perform a bit better than Vallejos when thinned more, they can handle being thinned a lot and still dry level and this allows for thinner coats to be applied and this helps with the entire HS process overall.

Humbrol - yes, I've even used enamels for this process, and while it's definitely possible to have success I would basically recommend Humbrols only for a really extreme paint job like heavy winter whitewash or desert camo that will get very distressed, thus requiring very thin outer layers with lots of areas of almost no paint, which allows the water get to the HS. Otherwise, if you use them as a very opaque outer layer it is almost impossible to chip.

A final thought on HS, *time* is not a huge factor overall. HS will not really dry out if covered with the paint, yet it also stays protected so future issues are not a problem. I have successfully re-chipped areas as long as 3 months after the initial paintjob was applied over the HS, so it's very *time* flexible for our needs.

○ Stage One - the model painted - it is then given two even layers of HS. Layer one is sprayed first, then dried. Followed by a second even layer of HS, which is also dried. Painting can commence immediately afterwards, no need to wait further.

○ Stage Two - the whitewasch is applied and chipping can begin. Depending on the style of worn finish you are looking, you can go as opaque with the top layer as required to achieve the look you are after, but the resulting chips will be less frequent.

○ **more tips for HS whitewash success:**

• the opacity of the white paint will be the main factor in how your chips will look. The more opaque the finish, the sharper and harsher looking the chips will appear. The thinner the white paint, the smaller and more random the chips will appear.

• use the various brushes and scratching tools to create a wide variety of marks on the surface.

• sometimes it is best to make one crisp main scratch, then switch to the brushes and create chips around it.

• study wartime photos of heavily worn whitewashed vehicles closely, they are the best source for seeing how it was applied and worn away. Different campaigns, armies and theaters had different methods and intensity levels of combat. Some were painted white, and then repainted again later if the winter lasted a long time, such as seen on the Eastern Front. Look at all vehciles, not just the tanks for reference.

○ Stage Three - after the whitewash is applied and chipped, a filter layer was applied to tone down the bright white color to a more realistic shade. Pinwashes are then added to bring out the details, and also add some subtle streaks and stains with oils.

OIL PAINT RENDERING

In depth explanation of this new and powerful technique

OPR ORIGINS

What is in the name? During my studies for my industrial design degree, I learned that the term *rendering* is defined for illustration as maximizing a drawing's level of information for the viewer, which is often used to visualize a product's physical elements to a client. This is common with automotive and product design illustration practices. Thus *rendering* for the sake of modeling is an idea I decided to transcend from the design world into the hobby. The surface of a model, especially ones that see combat service can have a quantity of information that can be clearly presented to the viewer, and how to achieve this effort is made possible with the use of oil paints. By creating a palette of colors related to the model's paintjob, we can go back over every area of the painted surface and recreate, enhance, reduce, add contrast, fade...in essense rework to nearly any extent what we want the viewer to see in this concentrated effort to *render* out the vehicles painted surfaces.

○ Stage One - OPR starts with a palette of colors related to the model's paint job. Tones and special effects are then worked over with colors that enhance the area being painted. Here, I'm starting to darken the fender edges to show dirt build-up and rust.

○ Stage Two - blending is a key element to achieving success. The proper technique involves keeping the blending brush clean and nearly dry. The amount of oil paint applied should be very small so blending is quick and easy.

○

Oil Paint Rendering - Background

Over the course of the last few years, I had progressed with my use of oil paints for weathering a model to the point where I felt it was unique enough, was controllable and repeatable, and could be clearly defined and called a new technique.

I took to oil paints early on in my models because they exhibited certain key characteristics that helped me extract the most from my finishes. They have wonderful blending abilities, take a long time to dry creating the requisite window in which to maximize the effects, and they have a broad level of opacities that are very powerful for weathering effects. Once I realized the fundamental elements of this process, I felt it necessary to share this idea with the hobby because it is one of the defining methodologies of my work, which I could now pass along.

Indeed, it took me a few models to come up with the basics that could be divulged, discussed, practiced and implemented. The goal of this effort was to further streamline the weathering processes and add inherent flexibility into the finishes that would then become unique to each model. This is in contrast to following a set outline and all of the models tend to look the same over time -- something I believe (from observation) happens on a regular basis in this hobby. Too often the preset steps become monotonous, and the resulting finishes change little from model to model.

What this step, *oil paint rendering*, brings to equation is that it has a much broader level of inherit opacity that allows for a wide range of flexibility in how the model can be finished. Thus, by definition, the modeler becomes the determining element rather than the product, or technique, being used. This is a subtle, but key factor in progressing model finishes to the next level. And as such, I would have to label this technique among the more advanced ones. It won't happen overnight. It will take practice, patience, and effort to see the maximum results from its use, but I believe strongly that *oil paint rendering* is an excellent idea ready to be shared.

OIL PAINT RENDERING

○ 1 - start in a logical spot, apply the oil paint in small quantities. Here, I'm going to darken the turret edge along the areas of exposed Dunkelgelb so I apply small amounts and dark brown color.

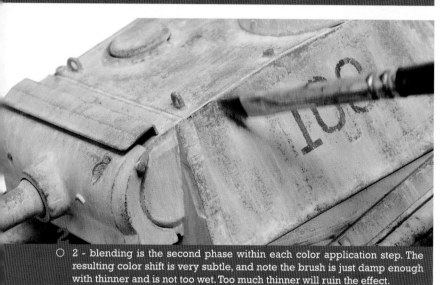

○ 2 - blending is the second phase within each color application step. The resulting color shift is very subtle, and note the brush is just damp enough with thinner and is not too wet. Too much thinner will ruin the effect.

tips for achieving blending success with OPR: ○

• not all blending motion is downward, get in the habit of becoming good with a stippling motion. Stippling is light quick tapping motion against the surface that helps to diffuse the color. I use it more often than vertical blending in fact.

• practice blending beforehand with various levels of thinner to see how the quantity of thinner on the brush affects the oils. Knowing how the oil will react gives you valuable information during the OPR process and the critical blending steps.

Having determined the value in *oil paint rendering (OPR)*, it now becomes necessary to break down the technique into a teachable method of application. Fortunately, the application process itself is simple and only requires a few basic tools, most of which we already own. Outside of the actual oil paints used, you will only need a few good quality brushes and a high quality odorless turpentine for the blending.

OIL PAINTS

The brand of oil paint is important, as is the thinner. It is best to avoid overly cheap products as the results will be hard to control and decidely inferior. And avoid hardware store thinners, they are chemically too *hot* for our needs. Overall high-quality oil paints are actually very economical because the amounts we use are tiny, so the tubes themselves will last for years. In fact, I am still using the same tubes of certain colors from when I first bought them years ago. I have used most store bought brands, as well as those created for the hobby, and here are my preferences:

502 Abteilung (MiG Productions) - These are my preferred brand of oil paints. They were designed for modeling with a slightly different manufacturing process to the art store brands, and I have found they have the best blending abilities for modeling, and work every time as intended. Combined with their *Odourless Turpertine*, the results are superior, and I cannot recommend them highly enough. The **502 Abt. Odourless Thinner** has a silky quality to it that really is noticeable, and I recommend it over other enamel based thinners, even the **MP** thinner. If it's not available definitely try to buy a comparable product. I also feel it is important to buy the oil colors that you need, and not be too concerned with the actual name on the tube, it is only a name, and not important to how or why we use them.

Winsor Newton - These are the art industry leader brand of oils, and thus are easily obtainable from any art store, have an excellent range of colors and are of superb quality. I use a few of their colors still, and they were my first brand of oils. They actually cost more that 502 Abt. in most cases, but without a doubt they are the standard quality brand for oil paints. I try to stick with those colors related to our weathering needs, but they also are widely used in figure painting, and have many uses beyond *OPR*, just like most oil paints.

Grumbacher - These are a more cost efficient alternative, they work well and have a nice range of colors.

Overall, I would simply state that price is relative to the

○ 3 - I work some dark brown in the upper armor plate joint to help separate the small panel.

○ 4 - Next begins a naturally repetitive process. I blend the oil paint into the panel, and I also drag some down to help create some initial subtle streaking.

○ 5 - Moving along the upper edge of the turret, I add dark spots to the exposed Dunkelgelb areas.

○ 6 - This is then blended quickly with a mostly downward stroke of the flat brush to create subtle streaks from those areas.

○ 7 - To help separate the cupola area a bit more, I add dark browns along it's edge.

○ 8 - I blend this color in following the contours and bring the color back to the rear of the turret edge. These early steps go very quickly, as I try to keep it simple.

○ 9 - Now I go back along the top edge of the turret with dark brown and black mix to help define this edge. I'm doing this to illustrate an area where the crew would frequently move along and over.

○ 10 - I blend this color in leaving just a trace of the dark tone along the sharp edge of the turret.

○ 11 - I want to further increase the contrast and add another dark brown-black layer of oil paint to the edge.

○ 12 - Switching to my flat blending brush, I carefully pull this color down as I blend it to fade the dark dirty edge more, illustrating a common crew sitting area.

tips for achieving success with the various blending brushes: ○

• each brush has unique qualities and it is good to know when to use which brush. Fine tipped brushes are perfect for fine streaks and getting into tight places. Flat wide rake brushes can be used for pulling larger areas downward, and also for stippling along close edges. An older softened angled brush is great for stippling and general downward streaking and blending.

• always have at least one new fine tip brush on hand when using OPR. Trying to make old brushes work past their prime is a cause for frustration and can do more harm than good at times. A new brush always gives superior results for fine streaks and stains.

quality of the paint pigments because the processes used to create each color do vary, so the more expensive brands are indeed superior, especially a color like white, which is very difficult to manufacture to a high standard due the pigment grinding process required. In general, buy those colors that relate to your models like tans, browns, greens, yellows, white, black, grey, and shades of orange, red and blue. These will cover the majority of the paint schemes used and it is good idea to build up a library of colors over time. Like I said before, the tubes of paint last a very long time, so in the end the costs are spread out over many many projects.

○ 13 - Using a more diluted amount of oil, I add darker tones to the armor plate joints. For thinner oil applications, simply dip the brush into the thinner first to make it wetter.

○ 14 - I then blend it using a sharp brush for added control and finer streaks as I pull the color down. I also use this brush to work the oil into the corners better.

○ 15 - Moving to the back edge of the turret, I want to enhance the subtle chipped area with some darker tones.

○ 16 - Switching to my flat blending brush again, I use a stippling motion to blend this oil into the edge and I leave just enough color to tint the area for a very subtle enhancement.

TYPES OF BRUSHES

There are only a few brushes that are needed for this technique. Again, price is relatable to the quality of the brush and I usually buy a mid-priced brand like **Loew-Cornell**© in most cases from my local art store. We do tend to abuse them rather quickly, so buy some good quality brushes but know they will need to eventually be replaced on a regular basis. I have a preference for Round #2 brushes for most of my work, because they hold a fair amount of paint when needed, and keep their sharp tip nicely over time. When working on the model, I typically will have one brush for each range of colors on my palette, so that means I have at least 4-5 #2 Round brushes ready to use for each project.

For the blending brushes I use three main types, the first one is called a 1/4 Filb Rake and it is thin, flat and has fine bristles for dragging and blending colors. The other main blending brush is a 1/8 Angular that is smaller and has an angled tip, which is very versatile in how it can be used to blend the oils. In addition to these two, I also have at least one clean new #2 Round brush on hand as well, it is always useful for fine streaks, or for those tight places that are hard to blend. A new brush will give the best results for those very fine details. I also keep a clean folded paper towel at the model's side too, this is for the constant removal of paint and/or thinner from the brush tips because keeping the quanities used on each brush is crucial to this techniques success.

17 - Now I want to enhance the more exposed areas of Dunkelgelb. I do this by adding an orche color to the these areas.

18 - I blend this in, careful to keep the color in the area I want to and not get too carried away with the streaking. I want just enough to create more contrast.

19 - Now I layer more dark browns in the same manner to help break up the whitewash a little more, note I'm adding a thinner mixture of oil so the results will be very subtle after these spots are blended in.

20 - I begin the blending with a stippling motion to diffuse the dark yellow brown tones across the white. I'll continue until they are nearly invisible.

my thoughts during the OPR application:

• I am constantly looking for ways to layer another effect upon a previous step. I do this because it provides a good barameter on the weathering as I move along. Once I determine enough has been done, I move along. This is an effective method to provide consistent results, and I never want to overwhelm any section over another.

• I constantly seek compositional balance in the overall visual appeal of the model, and within each section on the surface. Asymmetrical balance is also heavily considered; a small weathered section can be stronger than a larger area less weathered because they balance each other out, yet provides a more interesting end result.

OPR APPLICATION PROCESS

The actual process of applying the oil paint and then blending it out is very straightforward. In fact, it is exactly that direct -- apply the oil color needed to the model, and then blend it in. It is the requirement of the area and the colors used within the camo scheme that determine both the oil color to be used, and the opacity required. For example, if you are applying a dark brown shade to the edge of a fender with chips and scratches you are most likely showing a rusted metal finish. Or if you are applying a dark yellow oil color to a Dunkelgelb turret edge you are enhancing the color to show crew wear and usage.

○ 21 - With the white looking dirtier now, I want to bring some of the white back for more contrast and add thinned white oils in specific areas I want this effect.

○ 22 - After these spots are blended in the effect is a subtle contrast layer of white and Dunklegelb tones that add greater depth to the turret's side. The overall OPR effect is becoming clear by now.

○ 23 - Next, I want to add a much brighter and more opaque white to specific edges and areas of the whitewash to add more dimension to the paint, to increase the layered look of the finish.

○ 24 - I blend the remaining white oil using a fine tip brush and a vertical streaking motion, and with the turret side essentially complete, and I'm ready to move onto the next section.

more tips for success with OPR: ○

• It all starts with the color palette. Setting up the cardboard palette is the first important step, as this preps the oils for application by removing the linseed oil to a large extent. Why? It helps the oils to blend better, dry faster and to a matte finish. Shiny oil paint is not usually my preference.

• Proper blending is crucial, and it takes some practice and experience to achieve the desired results. Blending should be seamless, without visible strokes or sharp edges that end abruptly. It *must* look natural.

• Don't forget to study reference images for the many applied effects. Here readily available civilian vehicles can provide the right reference, especially construction vehicles. Look at aged rust streaks and how they blend out, look at faded paint and how subtle it can be, or how dust accumulates on top surfaces, the real world is perfect for this. I study trucks and heavily used cars all the time to keep ideas fresh for adding a new look to a weathered section.

Keeping the colors simple and related to the scheme of the model is the foundation of what the process is all about, so try not to overthink the concept.

The most important factors beyond color choice, is the amount used for each area. Generally, it is extrememly small for each step of the technique, and the photos above illustrate this nicely. *Less is more* is certainly a very applicable cliche when using *OPR*, and always maintain the concept of layers in your mind as you apply the colors. After blending, you can always go back and add more if needed, versus adding too much and then trying to remove them, which is nearly always a recipe for trouble.

OIL PAINT RENDERING

○ Initial Stage - at this beginning step, the paint actually looks pretty good, but there is so much that can still be done to it to add some life to the model. This is the end game of OPR, and why I spend so much time using it.

○ Final Stage - and after processing the turret side with OPR, it's much clearer as to its power and usefulness. It doesn't require much overall effort and the technique is quick once in a rhythm.

additional thoughts on OPR:

• having worked with oils for a few years now, they truly are a valuable and powerful tool. They have very little odor, and when used with odorless turpentine have near infinite applications and rarely do they harm the basecoat. I realized this a while ago, and have compiled my thoughts and methods on using oils into a repetitive process. Like any good technique, it takes some time to master, and always be open to the possibilities and power of an idea. Don't limit yourself with it. OPR is not just for adding a tint to a basecoat, or a quick rust streak, it can rework the entire model into a new visually attractive display that will draw the viewer in even more.

Besides the amount of oils applied, the use of the thinner is the other key to success. Here, the blending brush is best when almost dry. It does not take much thinner to make the oils turn into a wash and this not what we are looking for when blending. The blending process is one that requires the most practice, and the drier the blending brush the better. The blending brushes require constant cleaning and re-wetting during blending, so this is why the paper towel is important, it really comes into its own for creating the right level of blending brush dryness.

To prepare the blending brush I'm going to use, I quickly dip the tip of the brush into the thinner to get a small amount into the bristles, *but not to soak the brush*, and then dab it a few times on the paper towel to remove most of the thinner. I check it by lightly brushing it against my finger, there should only be a thin, visible, glossly line of thinner that dries quickly on the skin. This is about right for the amount of thinner needed on the brush, and you will quickly see if too much is used, which you can then wipe on the paper towel again. In fact, many times, the drier the brush the better, since a dry blend will create the gritty type of blend we are usually looking for. Vertical streaks is where the blending brush can be slightly wetter to help pull the color downwards.

I usually work from light to dark, and then top to bottom. But this is not a strict rule because once you get familiar and are experienced enough to know when and where to apply certain colors, it eventually becomes second nature. That is why I used this whitewashed Panther turret as my prime example, it clearly shows how the darks and the light colors play against each other, and how subtle the effects can be while still being very dramatic and visible to the viewer, without overpowering the finish of the model. All of which is critical to the success of *OPR*.

But it extends far beyond that. *OPR* can be used for nearly any type of finish on the model. It is perfect for rusting toolheads, staining paint, fade colors to show age and sun effects, enhance whitewashes and actually replace the mapping step if need be. It can replace filters and washes altogether if you are so inclined. It is all related to the amount of oil used, combined with the amount of thinner used. I believe *OPR* to be a 0-100% type of technique, and it has true untapped potential. My goal is to streamline the entire weathering process and maximize the paint finishes within each camo scheme. It can showcase a fresh combatant to an overused veteran tank. The power of *OPR* is just being delved into, and even beyond this first volume of TANKART, it will be the foundation process that I use for many more models that I create for the entire series.

○ Here is the Panther turret after the completed OPR effects and added spare track armor. Throughout the OPR process, I am constantly considering the overall appeal of the model, and the composition between areas and this helps to determine how much weathering to apply in each stage. My goal is always *artistic scale-ism* and to maximize each section of the model, while maintaining a strong visual harmony.

○ This photo of the near complete Tiger II model illustrates to a greater extent the shear volume of effects achieved using OPR. After painting and chipping with HS technique, all of the weathering effects seen on the painted areas were created with the oils. From the residual patches of worn whitewash, the myriad of rust streaks, to the dirty and rusty shovel head, the heavily weathered side fenders, the subtle faded Dunkelgelb on the front fender, the shadow tones from the missing tools, the dirty discolored areas around the hatch…etc. OPR is a very valuable and useful technique to render out these multiple effects at one time, creating a more efficient and harmonious end result.

PANZERBEFEHLSWAG

Pz Bef Wg Panther mit 7.5cm KwK42 L/70

Sd.Kfz 171

I had long desired to build a whitewashed Panther over a base coat of Dunkelgelb ever since I saw Phil Stutcinkas's original hairspray model of his Panzer IV Ausf. J back in 2007. There is just something very appealing about this color combination. It was one of those ultimate expressions of the craft and I wanted to push the limits of using hairspray to create all manner of wear and tear throughout the model. On top of which, the Panther has such an aura. So many of us love the look when they see one, its long barrel forever reaching out and the sloped sides and racy proportions all act together to create one of the best looking pieces of military hardware ever to set foot into combat.

How I approached this project was key. I had built only one Panther previously, the smaller 1/48 Tamiya Ausf. G kit, and I felt since so many brilliant Panthers had been built over time I needed to set mine apart. If I set such a goal, I knew I would push myself. That is the real trick to continually improve. For me, my models being such an artistic expression versus pure historical recreations, I always have a strong desire to seek new directions and new styles that will allow my inner creative side to flourish. A large part of what this book is about revolves around this concept.

Panther's are enormously popular subjects and I just didn't want to put another one out there. I wanted it to instantly be recognizable as one of my projects, and at the same time (and perhaps most importantly) give me a platform to really showcase what is possible with a scheme such as this. The opportunities for some serious weathering, illustrating my new OPR technique, and really lean on the hairspray process to develop a depth to the finish that I had a craving for. At the very core of how I paint and weather is the idea of building up layers and layers to maximize the achievable depth to a finish within realistic contraints. It is a process that I rework with every model, the steps always vary, and it is the honing of the techniques that allow each model to then step forward and not look back.

BACKGROUND

This project was originially started by a good friend, Daryl Dancik, who built up the older Tamiya Panther Ausf. G Late kit, then added a host of photo-etch upgrades and the always impressive Friulmodel tracks to create a stellar platform ready to finish. Once I saw the completed build, I knew I couldn't pass up the chance to paint it.

The construction process is nothing out of the ordinary, and Daryl built the kit to the instructions and then replaced the kit tool storage and bracket assemblies, front fenders, side skirts, and rear stowage bins with the requisite PE parts. He also took the time to add some subtle dents and battle damage into the fenders, side skirts, and rear stowage bins, which I would use as key points for heavier weathering later on. The barrel is the beautiful Aber metal replacement, and the Friuls tracks being the final touch. While the Tamiya kit is showing its age, once updated to this level it can hold its own against the newer Dragon releases and still gives a very fine representation of the breed.

After it was in my hands, I set about planning the various elements for the color scheme. Here is where I usually agonize the most. I tend to review a lot of reference material regarding what scheme to choose. Even though I had a good idea of what I was trying to achieve beforehand, I was still somewhat of cornered with the

○ Aerial view of the completed Befehls Panther Ausf. G with its distinctive "borrowed" replacement side skirt.

thoughts on how I wanted this model to turn out (my planning notes):

• I wanted the whitewash to be the dominate factor in the final look of this project, but I also wanted it to have maximum life and story telling attributes. I knew to achieve that I would have to put HS technique through its paces.

• when I received the model from Daryl, he had made three shot impacts on the frontal arc of the tank, and because of this I now had a viable reason to show a heavier weathered model as a result, because the tank had obviously seen some serious combat. Using this was useful to set the tone of the finish for the project.

• I don't like Panthers loaded up with any excessive gear or stowage, so with a mainly white overall color to the model, I had to come up with a few ideas to add color to it. The first was the spare tracks, I like the look of the turrets carrying lots of track armor and this was my first aspect to utilize. The other were the side skirts, but I was not sure how to treat at the start of the project. However, by the end I knew painting one of the side skirts in the 3-tone hard edge scheme this model should have worn underneath the whitewash was a proper homage to the fact this is a Late Befehls Ausf. G unit.

BEFEHLSPANTHER AUSF G

○ Many of the key visual items were replaced with PE parts--tool brackets, side skirts and rear stowage bins.

○ The front fenders are relaced with proper PE parts with added damage.

fact the model was built up as a very late-war Befehlswagen Panther Ausf. G, of which there were not many manufactured to begin with and finding specific reference on difficult. Now I confess the goal of this book is not solely focused on historical accuracy, I simply don't have the authoritative knowledge to author that way, but I still put forth substanial effort with finding a suitable paint scheme to use. So in the end I went with what I wanted it to look like based upon my research at the time, versus being 100% accurate to the unit and paint schemes used. I decided to show a SS Wiking Divsion unit and that gave me all the necessary elements for my proposed color scheme.

Ultimately though, I would have to concede the camo pattern error was not applicable because the SS Wiking Div. never upgraded their Befehls Panther Ausf. A tanks to the Ausf. G when it was deployed, and research discovered after the fact sums up most Befehls Ausf. G units were in some form of hard edge camo pattern. SS Wiking in fact soldiered onto the end of the war with their older tanks, so the scheme I'm showing is probably best replicated as a standard Heer unit command tank.

BASE COLORS

This is one of those fundamental steps of the project. The basis of the entire paintjob starts here and thus it is a very critical step, both in color choice and the quality of the actual airbrushing. The challenges are choosing a color suitable for the intentions and goals of the project and also to have a quality of finish to the surface so as all the weathering can take place on a smooth surface, which is always preferrable.

○

upgrading the Tamiya Panther Ausf. G kits:

overall the Tamiya Panther Ausf. G series are solid kits only requiring few changes to make current:

• aftermarket photo-etch upgrades are one of the best methods to improve upon these kits. A quality set like the Aber one goes a long way to replacing the simplfied plastic parts.

• while the 1-piece vinyl kit tracks are quite nice for the medium, swapping in a set of Friulmodel metal tracks substantially improves this important element of the Panther with its very prominent track sag.

• the rest of the kit measures out quite well and the outline is very convincing. The best part of the Tamiya kit is that it builds up very easily, which means less time spent gluing parts together and more time that can be spent adding said upgrades to model. Because the kits are still widely available, or kept in many of our stashes, this means it is still a viable option for a high-quality Panther project.

tips for creating that used-in-combat look:

• Panthers are great tanks to show empty tool brackets with, and the idea is to leave a smattering of tools in, and the rest empty. It's best to keep critical items such as the fire extinguisher in place. The side skirts and front fenders were also prone to constant contact and receive minor damage as a result. PE parts are the best way to replicate this battered look as seen here.

• The Tamiya kit has very smooth plastic, so it's a great idea to add a roughened layer of Mr. Surfacer to the plastic and then sand it back when dry to recreate a subtle armor plate texture.

○ Adding the armor texture and replacing the gun tube as easy enahncements to make on this kit.

BEFEHLSPANTHER AUSF G

paint callouts for the Panther project:

• **RED PRIMER:** I prefer a nice out-of-the-bottle choice. I like how *Vallejo Model Color Cavalry Brown 982* looks with a few drops of *Flat Red 957* added.

• **GREY PRIMER:** I prefer to keep this color warmer and darker to separate it from Panzergrau. A great choice is *Tamiya XF-24 Dark Grey* mixed with a few drops *XF-69 NATO Gray*, plus a drop of *XF-7 Flat Red*.

• **DUNKELGELB:** I have a few choices depending on the project, and because I was covering this one with a whitewash, it was a good idea to go darker underneath. For the Panther I used *Tamiya XF-60 Dark Yellow* with a few drop of *XF-55 Deck Tan* to cut the greenish tint down a little.

• **CAMO BROWN:** Camo colors always look best with a drop of the base color added, so I mix a few drops of the Dunkelgelb above to *XF-79 Linoleum Deck Brown.*

quick ref:

• RED PRIMER:
Cavalry Brown 982
Flat Red 957

• GREY PRIMER:
XF-24 Dark Grey
XF-69 NATO Grey
XF-7 Flat Red

• DUNKELGELB:
XF-60 Dark Yellow
XF-55 Deck Tan

• CAMO BROWN:
XF-79 Linoleum Deck
Brown

Because I knew I was painting a winter scheme, it is better to utilize a slightly darker than normal choice for a light base color such as Dunkelgelb. Contrast is more important than the actual specific color (ie. being absolutely historically accurate), and the final result will be dominantly white with heavily worn areas showing the base colors and it helps to have a stronger level of contrast.

The painting process starts off in a rather straightforward manner. After the model is primed with the Mr. Surfacer 1200, I spray the German red and grey primer colors as shown in the photos at right--these acting as the first layers of paint chip colors. Believe me, while it seems like a lot of work, it is very beneficial to build in your paint chip colors at these initial painting stages when using the HS technique, and is the main reason why I adhere to using this method throughout many of my models now.

Using the process that I describe in detail in the earlier chapter on the hairspray technique, I add the HS to the model and then spray the Dunkelgelb base color, on top

○ Stage One - primer layer via Mr. Surfacer 1200.

tips for achieving quality red and grey primer colors :

• I choose to paint the red primer as actual. I do this for the reason that I produce the red chips via the hairspray method, so it makes sense to start with it as the first color layer.

• I tend to lean towards a more true red and slightly brighter color because when the chips are very small they remain visible and look like red primer. Too dark of a color choice and the chips will look more like rusted metal than red primer.

• It is well known that German main gun barrels were primed in a heat resistant dark grey primer. I choose to have this color a "warmer" tone than Panzergrau (which I tint slightly cooler with blues). Thus I add a drop of red to the grey to give it this tint.

of which, I spray the Camo Brown color in the intricate SS Wiking criss-cross pattern. From here I spend a lot of time chipping and scratching in a very careful manner since I want some decent wear and tear. However, because this was a very late-war tank that had a short service life, albeit very intense, (and under rather extreme conditions late in 1944 and into early 1945), especially as an Eastern Front combatant that I am choosing to show it, it is a mix of harsh wear in an intense combat zone, plus some minimal wear in lesser used sections.

During the initial painting, I also take the time to add the first layer of turret numbers. As was somewhat common for German tank units, when they were depleted from combat losses they reorganized and often the tanks were renumbered accordingly, so here I add an earlier style command tank number to the turret sides (I will then add a different one during the whitewash phase). I almost always use the Eduard vinyl number spray masks whenever possible, same with the Balkenkruz emblem, which was a standard style on most Panthers. I find spraying the markings results in a more authentic look and allows for a slightly faded effect, which looks better in-scale to my eyes than decals or transfers. Often decals and dry transfers are so opaque and the whites and blacks so perfect, they take on a toylike appearance to me. Sometimes they are unavoidable, but in general, armor with large areas of flat plates allows for a greater usage of vinyl masks, thus I take advantage of them whenever I can.

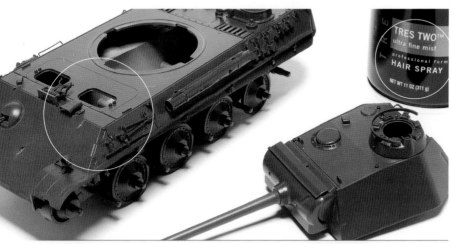

○ Stage Three - model is covered with two even layers of HS in preperation for the base colors.

tips for achieving quality hairspray layers:

• move the HS quickly, do not linger in one spot. You are really applying a heavy mist layer, letting that dry then applying one more. Use a hairdryer set on low heat to speed up the drying process.

• you can actually see it when it is applied properly, it look as above with an even dry glossy sheen to it. It should be dry to the touch when ready.

Stage One - basecoat and camo pattern successfully executed.

Stage Two - chipping starts around areas of high wear and tear, keep it logical.

Stage Three - use a variety of brushes and tools to recreate the chips with.

Once I had completed the lengthy chipping and scratching process on the Dunkelgelb and Red Brown colors, where there were larger chips and scratches I went back over the center of these with a dark charcoal grey/brown paint to illustrate exposed metal. I kept this effect to a minimum and confined to the sharper edges where it was likely to happen.

Now is the time to hand paint all of the small details like the tools, spare tracks and tow cable. Another important note to mention--notice that I painted the rubber tires after all of the chipping is completed to ensure they are crisp and look uniform, and don't suffer any unwanted damage from the chipping process. It's much more efficient that way then trying to keep them perfect and doing touch up painting afterwards.

WHITEWASH

With the base colors applied, first round of markings added, details painted, everything properly chipped and scratched, I can now add another layer of HS and then the main layer of whitewash using Tamiya XF-2 White as my preferred color of choice. I add a few drops of XF-55 Deck Tan to dirty the bright white color slightly. This is a subtle addition that I use in my whitewashes, which allows for more contrast with the subsequent mapping step giving the finished result slightly more depth without using filters in between to dirty up the white paint. It's more of a process preference than anything else, but worth sharing nonetheless. It becomes more apparent after a round of mapping, and I'll discuss that in greater detail later on.

For the whitewash layer itself, I spray the model with a varying degree of opacity, concentrating more white in areas

tips for chipping success with the HS technique:

• when working with HS and an opaque outer layer of paint such as with the first part of this project, it is best to start at a sharp edge or joint to get the chipping going. Usually once the chips start, it is relatively easy to keep it going. Any trouble spots can be helped along by making very small scratch with a hobby knife.

• wet only the section you are working on. It is not a good idea to leave water sitting on areas where you won't work on because it might potentially lift the top paint off if left unchecked.

• I typically don't use any varnish barriers between HS layers because I've yet to encounter an issue with lifting up lower paint layers after they have been chipped once already. The nature of the process already removes what HS is exposed, so the danger of more chips occuring is minimal, and honestly, if it does happen it can be easily worked into the overall finish. I'm not a fan of varnishes regardless because they alter visual paint effects after they are achieved.

○

thoughts after the first round of painting and chipping:

• at this stage the model has started to present itself as a combat veteran. The first round of chipping went well and with the details painted and markings applied, it's starting to look the part. I'm very happy with the tone of the darker Dunkelgelb, because I know once I spray the whitewash on top it will greatly diminish the strength of this color.

• the error in the camo pattern was discovered at about this stage, and I was in no mood to start over with a 3-tone hard edge scheme. So I knew in my head success would directly depend on the quality of the whitewash and how well it made the model valid in the end. I made double certain my two even layers of HS I applied below was consistent and even, I had a lot of chipping ahead.

that would naturally have a harder time being worn away. After I cover the model once, I then go back over and begin to add various patterns and streaks with the white to give the look of a more improm-prtu field applied whitewash. These elements really give the impression of a non-factory paintjob lending the model a more authentic appearance. The best part is nothing has to be perfect, the following steps of chipping and mapping will further enhance the whitewash. Note that I also allowed for a fair amount of overspray, especially on the road wheels and the tires. They were obviously not masked in the field, so this is a nice detail to represent accurately.

WHITEWASH - CHIPPING
Now the really fun part happens next with the chipping and scratching of the whitewash. Here is the defining stage of the paintjob, so it is important that I take my time and ensure a quality chipping job is performed. To repeat, the process is rather straight-

○ HS round two, the most important step of the project was the whitewash stage up next.

○ All the accessories were sprayed with white at the same time, overspray was intentionally added for authenticity.

tips for airbrushing the whitewash layer:

• white is actually a great color to spray in this manner. It is very easy to see where it's going, and how transparent the layer is. Opacity variation is important for visual appeal and easy to achieve.

• when using HS and Tamiya XF-2 White, thin the paint with water. This ensures the chipping is much easier to succeed with. Lacquer thinner simply adheres to strong to the surface making chipping very difficult, if not impossible.

• add a drop or two of XF-55 Deck Tan to the White to tone it down a little. This is important for the contrast you want to achieve between the base white, mapping more fresh white, and adding whiter patches for the maximum possible visual appeal of the whitewash layer.

○ Chipping is started one section at a time, and I work to create gradated chips across the whitewash.

chipping, chipping, and more chipping (and some scratches for good measure too):

• from my reference images, I had a very clear idea of the style of chips that I wanted to achieve. I was after a fine range of chips that gradated naturally from the high wear and tear areas to almost none in the hidden sections of white paint. To do this required my scruffy #4 round brush shown at left. The worn bristles had a soft end to the tip of the brush, yet they were strong enough to maintain a good level of control.

• areas where the crew frequented, like the hatches, were worked over to illustrate how their clothes and shoes would wear away clear areas of whitewash. And because of the myriad of sharp edges of the Panther design, it was a straightforward process to scrub along the sharp edges to start the chips, and then gently work my way along each section. Anywhere that I wanted a more severe chip or scratch, I would utilize the shorter bristle brush, or grab the toothpick to make the mark.

• I always work a natural motion that would replicate the marks in real life, so side-to-side for those along the hull side, and a gentle circular motion for the top surfaces to create a diffused effect.

tips for chipping continued:

• it helps to go over those same areas that were chipped previously because of the effort done prior to illustrate the layered chips, all of which is part of the master plan.

• once the process is underway, it is easy to get into a rhythm and this helps to achieve a cohesive effect. I try to complete at least one full section of the model at any given time on the bench to avoid the stop/start look to the chips.

• any items like tools that will get used often should show signs of more wear of the whitewash.

• my goal is to keep a constant watch on the amount of chipping, and I want panels where the crew work on to be clear and interesting sections for the viewer. The main hatch panel is a prime example of where I will focus this effort.

variety of size and style important:

○

• combat photos clearly show a wide variety of worn chipped areas. They were almost always focused on readily accessible areas. For example, the lower turret edge is constantly being kicked by crew working and moving about, and the side skirts are very exposed during the tanks travels and in this case received hits from small arms fire. All of these areas are key spots to show heavier chipping. Note: the sideways marks along the turret and side skirts were made with a sharper tool.

○ The chipping is now completed with each area receiving great care to show how it got to this point.

49

forward and simple, but it does require a deft touch and knowledge (or practice) with what style of chipping brush will yield what type of results. I chose my heavily worn #4 round which gives a nice scrubbing effect without being too stiff and this helped to create a lot of the finer chipped areas such as those around the hatches to show a more gradual gradation of the chipped whitewash.

To achieve success with this effort, I found it immeasurably helpful to study close-up photos of wartime whitewash finishes of combat units in the field. Thankfully, there are plenty of books available with good photos of such vehicles and I kept them handy. I won't be including a bibliography with this series, but I found some great winter war images in the **JJ Fedorowicz** title *SS Armor On The Eastern Front* by Velimir Vuksic, and there is also a healthy number of good reference images in the many **Concord** *Eastern Front* titles as well.

Without these reference photos at hand, it would be far more difficult to replicate a natural and authentic looking finish. Being able to clearly see how the chips and scratches look

thoughts on transitioning from the painting to the weathering stages:

• I maintain a separation between painting and weathering for a couple of reasons. I focus my efforts on getting all the painting completed first and out of the way before I start to really weather the model. I tend to think clearer about my processes this way and have a more linear progression throughout the project.

• the first two weathering steps should be the most subtle overall. The pinwash and filter are two elements that are used to add the initial definition of the details, and create the tone of the paint colors that give the model its in-scale look. Freshly painted camo tends to be bright with high contrast, and military vehicles used in combat, or intense training, don't exhibit this characteristic. The practice of complimenting the colors with a good pinwash and filter help set the base for the rest of the project.

○ The outer "newer" turret numbers after applying with an airbrush and Eduard vinyl masks. They were chipped with the HS technique.

○ The model at the filter stage. A simple single overall filter layer was applied to even the colors before the weathering starts.

○ A close-up of the contrasting spare tracks and how I used additional brighter white to increase their visual appeal.

tips for achieving depth with the whitewash and enamel mapping:

• I use both enamels and acrylics for the mapping stage. I'll explain enamel mapping first:

• enamels work best for blended effects, or those that require more diffused results. I'm often adding subtle layers of stains upon stains to the whitewash to make it look more like the crew applied this camo by hand. I want that "human" look to it, and the enamel mapping is perfect for this process. The results are very easy to achieve success with.

• you can begin to quickly see the way this is being executed in the two photos at right, in comparison to the previous images, the whitewash is very montone and by processing it in this manner it springs to life. Using the Humbrol Matte White for this effect allows for a lot of time to create each mapping effect exactly how I want it to look without drying too fast on me. I can work efficiently and make any corrections easily with the thinner.

○ Stage One - mapping with enamel to add streaks and stains within the whitewash. Paint the effect by hand first.

on the real tanks and half-tracks is how I determine the intensity of the chipping I apply to the model. Remember my adage is *artistic scale-ism* and this is the constant that helps to keep the weathering in check.

With that in mind, I work my way around the entire model chipping all the accessories, wheels, the main gun barrel-- going over every area completely. It does take a fair amount of time, but the results speak for themselves. To try and recreate this look by hand painting is nearly impossible, so HS really is a key tool for creating such an intricately chipped finish.

Next up, I apply a single filter layer to even the tones of the model somewhat using an

○ Stage Two - blend the painted enamel mapped effects to show runs, bleeds and streaking of the whitewash. **51**

thoughts on 3D micro chipping highlight edges:

• this is a relatively new technique that requires a deft touch and quality paint brush to have success with. The goal is to illustrate the top chipped paint layer has dimension to it, or in other words catches the light making it look three dimensional. However, it's very easy to overdue.

• the key is to use thinned paint and a new brush. I prefer #2 round tip brush and use my Optivisor to really see what I am doing. Trying to do this with the naked eye (especially for older modelers) is far too risky. My goal of effects rendered *in-scale* are always in my head with this step because it can have a very visible result. I focus my efforts mainly along the upper edge of the chipped paint areas to maintain a consistent light source.

○ The road wheels all received attention with both acrylic and enamel mapping. I liked the results enough to avoid using heavy pigments to cover it up in the end.

Ochre color for gray basecoats. I also apply the outer, or new, turret marking number representing a unit reorganization had happened. Again, I turn to the Eduard vinyl masks and airbrush the markings on. I spot spray a quick HS layer underneath each area first, dry it, then spray the markings themselves and now I could chip them to blend into the rest of the finish very easily.

MAPPING

One of the key steps in a quality whitewash paintjob is the mapping stage. While it is rarely discussed, it is a powerful step that gives much needed life to certain types of schemes such as this one. The basic idea is to add random areas of more opaque top color (in this case white), and this adds much needed depth and visual interest to the whitewash. Again, this is a rather simple and easily achieved process that only requires a quality brush (I prefer #2 round), and some white acrylic paint thinned to about the same consistency as you would for airbrushing. The Vallejo Model Air paints work great for this step because they are near perfectly thinned in the bottle to what we need for mapping. In this case, I will actually do both acrylic mapping and enamel mapping because with the different properties I can achieve different effects.

I start by using the white acrylic and hand paint on more opaque white patches, streaks and stains to the main model finish. I keep the effect concentrated to areas that would retain more of the whitewash over time, such as around joints and the myriad of details on the surface. The execution process is a bit similar to how you apply a pinwash and where, but it's spread out over a larger area. I then use the same #2 round brush and paint to add a few highlight edges along the chipped areas and this lends a slight 3D effect to the whitewash as well. But I'm cautious not to apply this effect everythwere, I keep it minimal yet noticeable. I add highlights to only the upper edges to illustrate light catching the edge of the paint. Keeping this technique *in-scale* is paramount!

Next, I switch the paint and my brush to Humbrol enamel Matte White and repeat the process, working to add more specific effects more along the lines of stronger visible streaks and stains within the white paint. This is very noticeable on the mapping of the road wheels and side skirts. Areas where the white would clearly bleed or run when first applied. Because of the enamels blending qualities I can use some thinner and help blend out some of these streaks to make them look more natural. I used this process to good effect on the side skirts, gun cleaning tube, turret sides and road wheels.

○ The whitewash runoff is created during the mapping stage and uses the natrual shape of the armor.

tips for achieving quality mapping effects:

• I'm always considering where I can add some subtle extra mapping effects. The model will give up clues and here I use the broad rear plates and stowage bins to show some extra whitewash stains and bleeding of color. Whitewash is typically a distempered paint that easily wears off over short periods of time, combined with hasty application process in the field gives us lots of opportunities to express this style of finish.

• focus the effects of whitewash runoff from obvious collection points where the paint would have gathered around when rapidly applied, such as the side skirt mounts seen above. Below, I use this technique on areas where the paint was sprayed heavier in a spotty appearance and then it bleeds off over time. It now becomes very apparent why toning down the white in the beginning pays dividends later on when adding bright white mapping paint to the surface. This is key to achieving success with mapping.

○ Key areas of runoff add tons of visual interest with just a few quick applications.

thoughts on focusing on certain aspects to attract the viewer's attention:

• nearly every model has a few areas or unique features that are perfect to address with greater attention to detail. Panther exhausts are definitely one of these key areas and I wanted to really illustrate them in a strong fashion with a layered worn off visual effect.

• these extra finishing ideas help reinforce the story of the model. Utilizing the early planning stages to identify these focus areas creates a more efficient and harmonious finishing process. It also takes full advantage of the technique you intend to use, such as the HS process on this model. I wanted to maximize the chipped paint on the exhausts and working it in from the beginning helped me to achieve that desired look.

• combining historical accuracy along with artistic intent is the cornerstone to the models in this series. I'm constantly looking at reference, looking back at the model and then determining where I can improve or enhance certain areas. And sometimes even if you know it will not be a highly visible area, or will be obscured later on with another effect (ie. adding pigments), it is good practice to be complete and thorough over each section of the model. In today's age of powerful DSLR cameras, it is common for the lens to pick up details we miss with the naked eye. I check my photos often to see if the camera sees something that I may have overlooked.

EXHAUSTS

The Panther exhausts are a unique feature of this tank and due to their exposed location are perfect for some extra attention. Because of the high heat element present both metal and paint take a beating and like the rest of the model's paintjob I built the layered finish into the painting from the start. I wanted to showcase a subtle variety of tones that illustrate both red primer and rust discoloration and I do this by layering HS in between each color so I can create a worn out patina effect on each pipe.

I actually repeat the first coloring process twice to render as much coloring depth on them for their small size as possible. I then add more HS and spray some Dunkelgelb that eventually gets heavily chipped to keep as much of the under colors exposed. This is seen in Stage One photo at right. Plus, I add some initial rust streaks as well, over which I will layer another HS layer so I can paint the white (the main whitewwash layer described previously). After the whitewash is applied, I chip it off until it matches the rest of the model's finish. As

○ Stage One - initial red primer and rust coloring to build up the first steps with the exhausts.

○ Stage Two - after the whitewash is applied, begin to increase contrast and darkening from soot.

○ Stage Three - use mapping in the white areas to further add layered depth to the paint, and then add some more rust with OPR.

the rest of the model's weathering progresses through the filter, pinwash and mapping stages I attend to the exhaust treatment at the same time. I add dark soot stains along the top edges and down the sides, and then the last layer of rust streaks and stains complete the exhaust painting. The final results are seen in the Stage Three image at the left.

PINWASH

At this point in the painting, I have the model entirely chipped, scratched, all the little details attended to and now I can begin the weathering of the paint. I first need to create a pinwash color that is unique to the model and compliments the tones of how the colors are heading, and as you can see it is a necessary to work with the warm dirty white paint that I've achieved to this point. I take a few of the new AK Interactive washes and mix up a pinwash color that is dark dirty brown with a hint of ochre coloring to it. Once ready, I attend to the execution of the pinwash phase. I much prefer this to airbrush shading since the it has superior control and works better to enhance the molded detail on the model. To complete the pinwash stage, I apply it with a #2 round brush and starting in one section I work my way around adding the wash to every panel line, molded detail on the surface to create a soft shadow effect, which works to pop the details off the model better

○ The main wash color was created from mixing the above AK Interactive fluids together into a new color.

for the viewer. I like to maintain a subtle approach now, then deciding to darken certain areas later I work my way through the weathering. While I'm applying the pinwash I also like to begin to add the first round of streaks to those details that would most likely create such an effect, usually tool bracket mountings and so forth.

OPR

With the model at a very convincing stage in the weathering, I can now turn my full attention to the main technique that will see the model to completion--OPR. However, because I used this model for the subject in the earlier chapter on how to use OPR, I won't get to detailed with it in this chapter. I start by creating my oil palette on scrap cardboard focusing on those colors related to the model 's paintjob, which ranges from white, most of the light tans and medium browns to the darker rust and dark brown tones. Some colors are staples like white, black, shadow brown, raw sienna, burnt sienna,

○ The pinwash is a key step in the beginning of weathering the paintjob. I use it to define the myriad of molded details, and also to begin adding some early stains and streaks in the paint.

---

tips for achieving success with the pinwash: ○

• a pinwash is a unique wash application designed specifically to enhance the models molding details and panel lines/joints. It is not an overall wash, but rather it is applied with a fine tip brush directly to each detail to create a soft shadow effect. Thus a fine tip #2 round brush is perfect because it holds a good amount of wash, and its sharp tip gives us maximum control of where the pinwash is applied.

• typically a pinwash is created from enamels or thinned oils, and this flows easily over an acrylic basecoat without harming it. The first layer should be adequate to provide the necessary shadow effect, but not overwhelm or clash with the base colors. Later on in the weathering, heavy washes are applied to enhance specifc areas like engine hatches. Any excess is blended after it has dried for a few minutes with a clean blending brush and thinner.

○ OPR starts with the defining of the surface details and paint wear and tear. Here, rust streaks are painted on the older scratches.

○ Blending is then used to reduce the effect to create a better in-scale appearance. Good quality brushes really do make the entire process much easier and more successful.

57

○ **thoughts on weathering a winter whitewash Panther:**

• at this point the weathering is now becoming very specific. I'm using OPR to go over each area and render out the effects appropriate for the spot I'm working on. I enhance the spare tracks to show more rust bleeding through the whitewash, I'm adding wear and tear to the engine deck details, and around each hatch I'm laying down dark colors to show how the crew hands would discolor the open edges during their daily routines.

• I actually work over the three shell impact spots in as minimal a process as possible, because extreme battle damage can easily overwhelm a model giving it a toylike and unrealisitic appearance. It is that constant balancing act, knowing when to enhance certain spots also means knowing when to downplay others. I often step back from the model to view from a farther distance to see if my processes are going in the right direction, and by using oil paints I can reduce any effect with thinner and a clean brush if I feel it is too much. This type of adjustability within OPR adds confidence as well.

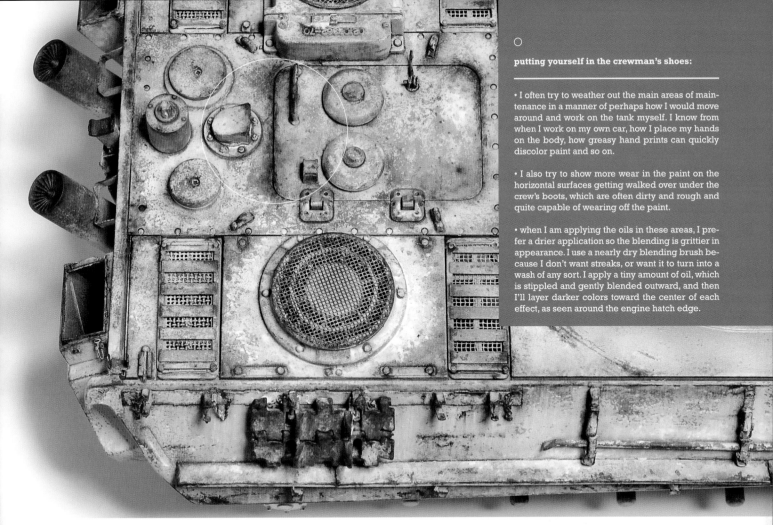

• I often try to weather out the main areas of maintenance in a manner of perhaps how I would move around and work on the tank myself. I know from when I work on my own car, how I place my hands on the body, how greasy hand prints can quickly discolor paint and so on.

• I also try to show more wear in the paint on the horizontal surfaces getting walked over under the crew's boots, which are often dirty and rough and quite capable of wearing off the paint.

• when I am applying the oils in these areas, I prefer a drier application so the blending is grittier in appearance. I use a nearly dry blending brush because I don't want streaks, or want it to turn into a wash of any sort. I apply a tiny amount of oil, which is stippled and gently blended outward, and then I'll layer darker colors toward the center of each effect, as seen around the engine hatch edge.

The hatches are perfect areas to illustrate differences between adjacent panels.

BEFEHLSPANTHER AUSF G

thoughts on working with oils as a primary weathering product:

• in recent years we've had a steady introduction of many new unique weathering products, but I continue to rely heavily on the usefulness of oil paints. Besides their great blending properties and the forgiving length of drying time, they also don't have too strong of an odor, especially when combined with odorless turpentine. This is in stark contrast to enamel based products whose odors are powerful and intrusive to say the least, and can be harmful over long periods of continued use. Oils do little harm to any basecoat as well, giving us a wide margin of protection against ruining a paintjob.

• oil paints also have a very long shelf life because of the small amounts required, they last over the course of many models. I am still using tubes of oil paints that I purchased years ago. This makes oils very efficient and cost effective products.

• the complexity of using oils is also very basic. Once the palette is generated, a simple application of the color and then blending it out is really all there is to it. The quality of the brush, style of tip, type of blending stroke, and the amount of thinner used are the four main aspects that affect the outcome. Practice and experience are all that is left.

light mud and dark mud, all of which I usually find a good use for on each model. The rest of the oil color choices follow the model more closely.

You can see the outcome better by studying the images on these pages the results of the OPR process. In essense, I worked my way around the entire model, starting at the left front fender and enhanced each detail and section of the surface with the oils. I created all manner of stains, fades, streaks, and shadows to further render out the model. Some areas such as the spare tracks on the hull sides received considerable attention to distinguish them and provide a stronger visual contrast to the surrounding areas. Anywhere that the crew frequented and performed maintenance (especially the hatches) I paid extra attention to the surrounding paint and treated to give it the appearance of constant use.

○ Spare track armor was first "painted" the same manner as the other Friuls, with Blacken-it solution.

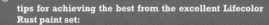

○ Simple metal hook track hangers were used to hold the links in place. They were made from cut brass rod.

○ The variety of rust tones are a result of extensively using the Lifecolor Rust paint set, it is perfect for this process.

SPARE TRACK ARMOR

I planned early on in this project to add the distinctive Panther turret spare track armor to this model as one of the main areas of constrasting colors to sea of whitewash. Often times this concept is achieved via some form of stowage items, but here I wanted to utilize the spare tracks more to convey this idea to the viewer. I already had done this to a certain extent with the spare track links mounted to the hull, which I illustrated to show they have been stored there for a while, at least before the whitewash was applied, so I wanted a somewhat altogether different result for the turret mounted track links. For this I used the Lifecolor Rust & Dust paint set to its maximum potential.

Because these spare tracks are all Friuls, I first go through the Blacken-it process to give them a proper basecoat coloring. Once they are dried, I applied the 4-color Rust paints from Lifecolor starting with the light yellow first and work my way all the way through to the dark rust shadow color. I use both a sponge and brush to paint the variety of tones, and as you can see, I spent some time altering the intensity between the various links to arrive at a subtle yet distinctive visual quality to them.

61

○ The completed Befehls Panther with the reclaimed side skirt and the heavy dark mud pigment application at the rear of the hull.

○ I kept the track color dark to further illustrate the winter tones and feelings of cold bitter fighting.

○

thoughts on the excellent Friulmodel metal track sets:

• I've long had a fascination with Friul tracks and use them whenever possible on any project. The added weight, realistic track sage, and durability during handling are worth the extra cost for me. But it was with the advent of combining them with Blacken-it (a model railroad metal burnishing chemical product) that I completely fell in love. The coloration process is superb and one of the most realistic finishes I've ever seen in scale. I've tried to replicate the results with paint and washes before, but I could never capture the gritty real look Blacken-it imparts on the metal.

thoughts on the final composition of the model:

• how the model looks at the final step is the result of the long painting and weathering process. What is built into the model during construction is then realized through the paint, and ultimately the weathering, which makes it a vital step in achieving success for the project. The composition of these elements is crucial and how the balance is arrived at are constant thoughts that never leave my mind as I'm working. I also look at how symmetry, or rather the lack of it, can really play its part too. I never paint one side the same as the other, I often use a simple side-to-side breakdown to make the model more interesting as you move around it. On the surface it seems like common sense, but it does require forethought and planning to create successful results from this idea. The side skirts are a superb example of this concept, I intentionally only added the colored one on the left, leaving the right hand side in the basic whitewash tones, and as a result the final compostion actually looks more natural and not forced.

The less colorful right hand side, still loaded with tons of subtle visually interesting areas.

63

These paints are more like a liquid pigment and dry to a very matte finish, and work great when heavily thinned with water and layer up with a variety of opacities.

TRACKS AND PIGMENTS

The actual amount of pigment application on this project was limited; one, because on the Panther it is so hard to see the lower hull through the overlapping road wheels, and two, I didn't want to hide the extensive winter painting efforts over said road wheels as I quite liked them with the simple wash and minor weathering. Thus, I confined the pigments to the rear of the hull mostly. I applied darker tones here to add further contrast to the white, and to show a dark wet permafrost earth that would be churned up as the tank moved along.

The Friul tracks were given a healthy bath of Blacken-it, which is my preferred chemical of choice to finish metal tracks with. After that step, I add the same pigment colors I used on the lower hull and set these into place with a rather substantial amount of dark brown and rust colored washes. I intentionally kept the track tones dark and quite ominous looking. I felt this range of colors on the model lent a real dreary desolate wintery feeling and this compliments the late-war last stand type of status typical of these subjects.

FINAL DETAILS

The model is at the final completion stage now. With the main tracks mounted for the last time, I also add the command antenna, tow cable, and side skirts. For some additional visual appeal, I repaint one of the side skirts to replicate the factory applied 3-tone hard-edge scheme that perhaps this crew used to replace one of theirs lost in the field. I painted it using the same layered HS technique as before, painting and chipping each camo color over the lighter toned Dunkelgelb, creating heavy chips and scratches that look distinctly different to the model's to further illustrate this piece was from another tank altogether.

○ Close up of the left side running gear and reclaimed side skirt. The myriad of effects were created largely via the HS technique.

thoughts for adding that final detail to complete the project:

• I knew I wanted to keep the model simple, yet create a strong visual statement at the same time. The Panther already has a ton of cool factor to it, so it didn't take much to enhance its basic appeal. The mantra of *less is more* is often quite true and by simply repainting one side skirt to look like it was from another tank is directly to the point, and a very efficient use of what can be done quickly and easily. I made certain that when I painted it, I changed the tones of the colors used, especially the lighter Dunkelgelb paint, and the style of the wear and tear as well to look like it too had it's own story to tell. I utilized the HS technique and some simple Post-it note masks to paint the hard edge scheme using reference images to ensure the pattern was accurate.

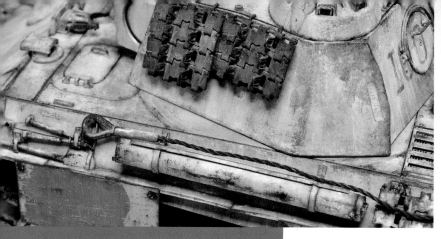

Sd.Kfz 171

Panthers are one of the mainstays of the armor modeling hobby, especially for the fans of WWII German Armor. The sleak profile, long powerful gun that was capable of destroying any Allied tank at most ranges give it a menancing reputation, and this is translated perfectly to the scale model world with modern kits and aftermarket products. There have been countless amazing Panther models built over time and I wanted to really do the subject justice. I am grateful to have been fortunate enough to be combined with the superb construction skills of my friend Daryl Dancik--the end result lived up to my original finishing goals that I set forth.

Two main factors were key to this success. The first being an extensive use of the Hairspray Technique, it really was the crucial painting element that allowed for the sheer depth to the heavily worn whitewash finish. I could not have created such a finish to this level of scale realism without HS in my opinion.

The other factor was the development of my new Oil Paint Rendering technique, which came to full realization on this model. Using oil paints as much as I do has really been a cornerstone of my work for years, and truly supersedes all other weathering processes for me, even pigments to a certain extent. Naturally, I still use pigments for the heavier dirt accumulations, but dust effects certainly come under my use of OPR now too. This technique is in its infancy and now that I have expressed it in a formal manner I feel it can spread through the hobby as a viable methodology for weathering, not just armor models, but all genres out there. I believe it to be a very powerful technique indeed.

PANZERBEFEHLSWAG

Pz Bef Wg Panther mit 7.5cm KwK42 L/70

PRIMER

RED & GREY PRIMER

1ST HAIRSPRAY LAYER

BASE COAT & CAMO

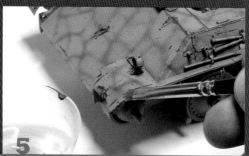

CHIPPING WITH WATER

2ND HAIRSPRAY LAYER

PAINTING WHITEWASH

CHIPPING WITH WATER

APPLY FINAL MARKINGS

FILTER

MAPPING

MAPPING - BLENDING

QUICK REF SBS

MAPPING DETAILS

CHIPPING 3D EDGE DETAILS

ROAD WHEEL MAPPING

PINWASH MIXTURE

PINWASH

OIL PAINT RENDERING

OPR - BLENDING

ENHANCED DETAILS

MORE STREAKS AND STAINS

EXHAUSTS

SPARE TRACK ARMOR

TRACKS & PIGMENTS

69

PANZERKAMPFWAGEN

Pz Kpfw Tiger mit 8.8cm KwK36 L/56

Sd.Kfz 181

Flashback to 2005 when it happened - the dawn of the super kit. Dragon upped the standard in the hobby with what can only be described as one of the biggest news items for the armor modeling crowd. They unveiled an all new-tool 1/35 Tiger I Initial Production kit, touted as a 3-in-1 all-inclusive wünderkit. Their marketing was relentless. No stone was left unturned, they claimed countlesss number of research and development hours had been invested into the project. It was as accurate a plastic model as had ever been made to date. Indeed, a new era had arrived and the price was a remarkable $35, including photo-etch details, turned metal barrel, partial interior, state-of-the-art link-to-link tracks, and more. The box weight was nearly 3lbs!

Like many people at the time, I was a skeptic. Up until then Dragon kits, while generally decent quality, had a very up-and-down history of poor fit, soft details and often required corrections to make accurate. No kit is perfect, but previous to the Tiger I Initial release building a Dragon kit was usually a challenge. On the other hand, we already had a great Tiger I kit range from Tamiya, I even remember discussing with friends how there was no way the new Dragon kit would out do the venerable Tamiya offering. How wrong we were. The day the new kit arrived, I opened it up to compare sprues with Tamiya's, and there was an audible silence as I stared in disbelief. Could this really be true? Had Dragon figured out how to produce a kit of superior quality to Tamiya? Well, the answer was a very loud--yes! And at an asking price that was even cheaper than the 20-year old Tamiya kit. Yes, I know a true Initial Prod. release was never tooled by Tamiya, but in the end that didn't really matter. There was a legitimate change in the pecking order for 1/35 armor models, and this was the kit that ushered in that era.

TIGER I INITIAL PRODUCTION

○ **a tale of two models within the same project:**

• every now and again, a project takes a lot longer to finish than originally planned for. This was just such a project, and it was a transitional piece whereby I developed new techniques that I knew would make the results far superior to my first efforts.

• a model is only finished when you want it to be, and I travelled with this one to EuroMilitaire where it medaled, but I was never satisfied with the outcome of the finish. Upon my return, I attacked the project with verve and completely redid the weathering.

○ The final result after nearly three years of work. This model had two distinct lives!

CONSTRUCTION EFFORTS

First impressions put in check, and accolades aside; how did the kit go together? Barring one issue I had with the fit of upper hull plate to the frontal armor, the kit, while complicated, was overall a huge leap forward for Dragon. The only real weakness of the kit is the instructions. There is a distinct gap between the quality of the plastic and quality of the instructions. In this particular case, the kit is billed as a 3-in-1, meaning you can build any one of three distinct versions. The problem is that Dragon insists on illustrating all the features into the instructions without declaring which parts are for which version. So you are left to your own wares about this. The problem is compounded in that reference material on the initial Tigers is difficult to come by, and there is no book that gives a clear idea of what was fitted, and when, to what tank number. Not to mention a few mislabeled part numbers, which only adds to the frustration. But the details are amazing, so you tend to forgive this issue and move on.

Because of the nature of the subject, this wasn't a quick build by any means. The Tiger I was an over-engineered beast of a tank, and Dragon captured that element perfectly, both literally and figuratively. Two areas, in particular, caught my attention. First, were the missing engine grille screens, which I used the Aber PE set for. And second, I decided to go with aftermarket tracks from Friulmodel. I gave up the accuracy of handed tracks for a set with hollow guide horns. Plus, the Friuls can be finished to a very high standard with Blacken-it.

The surface details of the kit are excelletnt, so I only added wing nuts to the top of the tool brackets along the edge of the upper hull, and added the raised cast two-digit number on the top of the mantlet. The rest of the kit is built straight from the box. All of the nice weld beads are molded in and everywhere you look the attention to detail is top notch.

I also set a personal challenge for myself to see how well I could reproduce what is likely the most popular and modeled tank kit in history. Never having built a Tiger before, I knew I was not up to speed on every detail and this would be a hindrance that I must overcome. It all starts with the bascoat...

PAINTING BEGINS

Normally a tank model is built complete and then painted as a whole, but here a little forethought helps to solve the problem of painting all of the overlapping road wheels. Instead, I paint them while still on the sprue, which I found easy, if not time consuming due to the quantity involved, to spray each wheel with the tire color first, then mask off the center using a circle template and spray the Panzergrau over this.

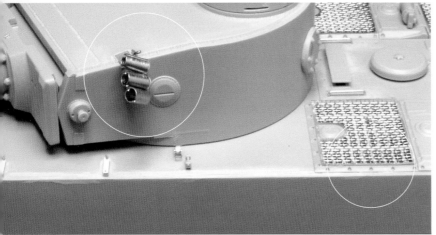

○ The kit includes the metal smoke dischargers, but new PE engine grille screens are required.

Next on the agenda was to decide on the actual tank I wanted to depict. I had made most of the necessary additions to the model to narrow down what few choices I had, and from this I chose tank number *111* in the end. Also, I had previously purchased a rare magazine from a Russian publisher called Frontline Publications specifically on the Initial Tigers from the 502 Abt. The book was not in English, but it did include English-language captions, which really helped. The Frontline Pub. book was the best source of early photos I could find and this helped a lot. Inside was also some nice color illustrations and from this I had all that I needed to precede with the painting.

One profile drawing of *111* stated it wore a two-tone camo pattern of RAL 7005 Mausgraü over the existing RAL 7021 Scwarzgraü base coat. I was skeptical of its accuracy, but

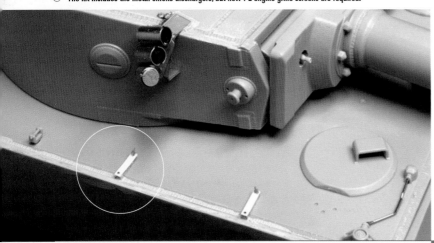

○ I replaced the cleaning rod brackets with styrene and Modelkasten wing-nuts.

○

thoughts on construction of the Dragon Tiger I kit:

• what was immediately clear when assembly began was the kit was a massive improvement in overall quality for Dragon, from the plastic itself to the general fit of the parts. The model is on par with the best kits on the market.

• Dragon loves to use sub-assemblies that get joined together, then fitted to another assembly, but this is often a difficult process and dry-fitting becomes a must. However, after a proper sequence is determined using the complicated instructions as more of a guide, the build goes relatively smoothly.

• The only area requiring any adjustments worth noting was the fitting of the upper hull deck to the hull sides. Here I found it tricky to get a perfectly flush fitment from front to rear, and there was a hint of warping that required some filler to finalize the joints. Mr. Surfacer was required to fill the joints along the top edge of the hull, but nothing too difficult in the end.

○ All the PE tool brackets are supplied in the kit, a fantastic addition for the price.

a clear photo of 502 Abt. Tiger number *112* showed this exact camo pattern, so that was enough justification for me to get started. I began by choosing my paint, **Lifecolor** in this case. They were relatively new at the time and I wanted to give them a try. The first color I laid down was UA 022 Dark Grey, which was to represent the factory base coat. I followed this by lightening the model with UA 029 Grey and also added some streaks down the vertical sides of the turret and hull in an attempt to imp-art an underlying breakup to the monotonous camo. Markings were next and I used a combo of spray masks for the 502 Abt. from Lion Roar, which included both sizes of the Mammoth logo. The Balkencruz was applied with Eduard spray masks and the ability to fade the markings at this level is the main reason I use masks instead of decals, which are always too opaque for my tastes. Once suitably marked up, I then painted the overlying cloud pattern of

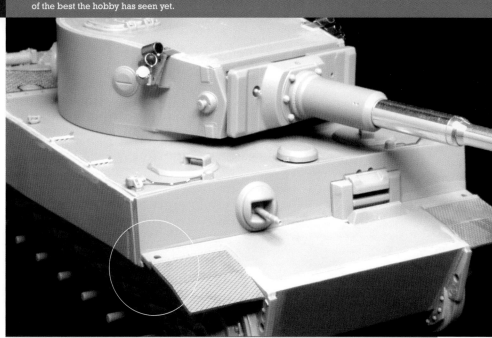

○ I chose the version with the textured front fenders, again these PE parts are in the kit.

paint callouts for the Tiger I Initial project:

• **PANZERGRAU (ORIGINAL):** I used Lifecolor for this project extensively, finding the colors very pleasing in-scale. *Lifecolor UA-022 Grey* is an excellent out of the bottle option for Panzergrau. I like the choice because it was plenty dark and had a reddish tint to it that shifts tones depending on the light source, looking bluer outdoors, which I think is a very close assessment to what we see in color film.

• **PANZERGRAU (LIGHTENED):** For lightening the general tones of Panzergrau, *Lifecolor UA-029 Grey* and *UA-034 Light Grey* combined provide a nice complimentary shift in colors with a hint of blue to them. This is lightened even further by using more of the UA-034 in the mix for the final camo pattern.

• **GREY PRIMER:** The Grey Primer in this case is actually the original Panzergrau color left unaltered and masked off during painting the lighter tones and camo pattern, creating a natural contrast.

quick ref:

• PANZERGRAU:
UA-022 Grey

• LIGHTENED PAN-
ZERGRAU & CAMO
PATTERN:
UA-029 Grey
UA-034 Lt Grey

Mausgraü with a mixture of UA 029 Grey and UA 034 Light Grey. In the process, I masked off the main gun to keep it in the darker gray color to represent grey primer. Next was to paint the tools and exhaust pipes with the appropriate colors.

Another incident of good timing happened again with this model. I had originally painted the exhaust with Humbrol rust tone enamels, but Lifecolor (always introducing new products) developed a specific series of paints intended to reproduce accurate rust finishes called Rust and Dust from their Diorama series. I was quick to buy a set and wasted no time re-painting the exhaust with these superb paints.

PAINT CHIPPING
A great trick to use for a unique paint-chipping look is when you have at least two layers of color overlapping each other, you can use a little paint thinner and a clean brush and gently remove the outer layer of paint creating very subtle paint chips in the process. The idea is to convey a look of worn paint in a controllable and subtle manner. In this case,

COLORI ACRILICI PEINTURES AC

LIFECOLOR

UA 034
FS 36251

net 22 ml

Light Grey
Grigio Chiaro
Gris Clair
Grau

○ Stage One - the first basecoat color is applied with Lifecolor UA-022 Grey.

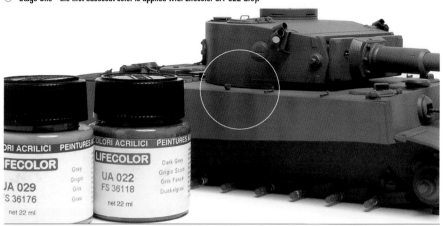

○ Stage Two - this is followed with the lightening of the general tones and some subtle streaking in the paint.

○ Stage Three - markings are applied via excellent Lion Roar PE templates and Eduard vinyl masks.

I used Vallejo's Airbrush Cleaner, which works well as a thinner/cleaner for both Vallejo and Lifecolor acrylics, and is just strong enough to rub off dry paint without causing too much damage. I am always nervous showcasing any technique that is of this type, so I strongly suggest a trial run before you work your own model in this manner. The trick is to keep the brush almost dry and do not put a lot of thinner on it. Keep a paper towel handy to dab the brush on frequently. I worked on every area of high use by the crew with this technique, the rear engine deck, turret edges and hatches, and the front hull around the crew areas. After all of this I carefully went back around and selectively hand painted some of the larger ones with layers of red primer and bare steel to add variety and show heavier use.

The next step was the turret numbers, which I used Eduard's Medium German Number spray mask set with a slight modification to the end of the number *1* to better replicate the font style in use at the time. The process was helped with the use of Tamiya tape for lining up the masks so the numbers would be painted on straight. As a further addition to the Balkencruz painted on previously, I made some thin masks with tape and added the black lines along the inside of each cross. This was a rare form of the national markings and I really liked how they changed the look of the model, even if it was ever so slightly.

WEATHERING BEGINS
With the main painting stages completed, I could now get on with weathering this tank. My first order of business was to apply a pinwash made with a Humbrol earth colored ena-

mel. Because the layout of the armor panels is actually rather simple, this step went quickly, and I will add much darker panel line washes in the later stages of the finish.

Next up was a major step in the process, applying the pigments. This was directly due to the complexity of the suspension and road wheel design, and I forced myself to treat both sides of each road wheel equally regardless of whether the surface would be seen or not. And let me tell you, a lot of the work is impossible to see once they were all mounted to the hull.

PIGMENTS, ROUND 1

Over time, I have developed an easy way to apply large quantities of pigments along the vertical edges of the lower hull. I start by placing the hull on its side. This has the obvious gesture of making a vertical surface horizontal. Now I can add dry pigments, as much as I want without worry of them falling off. To set them in place I add drops of thinner or fixer to the edges of the surface and let the capillary action flow the liquid throughout the area. What is great about this is that you can repeat this process many times. When I work with pigments, I do not use just one color, I make mixtures of a few

tips on painting tools and fittings while on the model:

• if you are new to armor modeling, this idea may seem strange at first. But I find it more efficient to paint tools and fittings like exhausts after base painting in an effort to avoid trying to glue parts to a painted model. In most cases they are quite visible and glue stains are very difficult to correct.

• a simple trick to avoid accidently painting the surrounding model is to cut small strips of paper (or use Post-it notes) and slide them under the tools as you paint them, thus protecting the model with a simple mask.

• it is always best to thin the paints for brush painting as well, paint in thin layers so the paint dries even and does not show brush strokes.

○ Details are handpainted in place.

○ Vallejo Airbrush Cleaner/Thinner works great for surface chips that do not go too deep.

• the technique of using a thinner to gently remove an outer layer of paint is a tricky one to discuss. It carries inherent dangers since it does not take too much thinner to cut through the paint. But that said, the effects itself are quite authentic and worth the effort.

• the goal is to carefully distress the outer most color, which uncovers a contrasting lower color, in this case the difference is between a lighter gray and darker gray whereby I want to remove the outer camo color to show wear and tear.

• once these areas defined, I then go back over larger marks and paint inside them to illustrate a variation in the depth of some of these areas providing a contrast and more story telling information.

• the trick to the process is to keep the chipping brush nearly dry of thinner and hardly use any liquid at all. Basically you are dry-brushing the surface with the thinner, gently scrubbing away paint in the process.

pigments in the tones I want to use. I create Light, Medium and Dark blends by varying certain pigment colors after I make the first mixture. I store these 3 colors in 35mm film canisters for use over many models. Once applied, this process adds a tremendous amount of depth to the area and looks remarkably realistic. The front and rear ends of the hull are also treated as well for complete coverage.

Overall, the pigment application process itself is straightforward -- with the hull on its side, I cover the area with the medium pigment first, add the light color along the upper third and then the dark color along the lower third and around the suspension arms. I then add the fixing agent to set them all in place, and finally dry the area off with a hair dryer set to low heat. I usually add some more pigments on top for added depth, and then really get things dirty with dark washes and stains around the moving parts.

After each side had been so treated, I added tiny stains to the sides by flicking various dark brown and black wash mixtures with an old brush. This is an old-school technique for making random spots and stains that I use quite often to obtain that "gritty" appearance. From here I turned my attention to the road wheels. I worked on one wheel layer at a time applying pigments and stains in a random sequence to achieve as natural of an appearance as possible. The pigments were applied in the same manner as the hull, and on some wheels, I would add more pigments to create some variety. Once each wheel was dry, I added various stains with dark oils to replicate leaking bearings, or recent maintenance.

○ Chipping was concentrated around hatches and along the sharp edges of the armor, anywhere the crew used frequently.

○ I worked the chips with a fine tipped brush to create a realistic worn effect in the outer camo color.

79

HEAVY METAL TRACKS

One of the more enjoyable parts of working with Friulmodel tracks is the way in which you can finish them. I love to use Blacken-it, which is a chemical etching and darkening solution available from specialty hobby shops and better-equipped railroad modeling stores. The process is rather straightforward, but there are some tips that can make it even easier, and almost foolproof. It starts with having some plastic containers with lids that seal tight. I prefer the small plastic bowl style found in the common grocery stores made by GLAD™. The small bowl size is perfect to fit Friul tracks into when they are rolled up, then they are filled about 2/3 with Blacken-it, or enough to completely cover the tops of each run. I close the lid, shake them for a few minutes and then let them sit until the liquid goes clear again. That is usually a good amount of time to give them that perfect dark brown rusty track color.

However, I was far from done. The basic color was set from the solution and now I can add the dirt and additional discolorations. I don't really do anything different when it

Lining up the turret numbers that are slightly modified to alter the font to match photos better.

tips for achieving success with layered micro-chipping:

• hand painting layered chips is a very common practice and yields excellent results. Once the basic shapes are determined in the first step, you can then paint inside the chips to show further wear down to the steel if desired.

• use thinned paints and fine brushes, plus an Optivisor if your eyes need extra help because accuracy is key to success. Paint from the lightest color to the darkest, and from outer to inner in that order, so the steel center color is the last one applied.

thoughts on the first steps in the weathering process:

• one of the most critical stages are the first weathering steps. These steps really help to define the tonal qualities of the model in its weathered state, thus, it is very important to choose the right colors, and start the process with precision.

• the pinwash is a key element to this equation. It is a highly accurate form of wash that defines all of the molded details present on the surface of the model. However, it is not the final color, it is only the initial tone to jump start the weathering. I typically chose a wash color related to the final dirt colors and complimentary to the model basecoat paint. With most armor, this is usually a medium brown shade that you want to be visible when dry, but not overwhelm the model right off the bat. Less is more here, and you can always add layers to it afterwards, which is normal procedure in the course of the weathering.

• on this model, I selected a medium grey-brown Humbrol that was thinned about 80% and then drawn over all details. I always use a fine tipped brush for accuracy and take my time, with any excess easily blended away with a clean brush after it has dried for a few minutes.

• filters are the next step, and this has the effect of toning the basecolors down a bit more and tinting them a little to better represent a vehicle in the field. The filter process starts to help the model look in-scale and not so toylike. You can add filters before or after the pinwash, that order is not overly critical.

• again chose a color that will be represented throughout the length of the project, so here I used a light tan shade of Humbrol thinned 95% and airbrushed over the entire model. I dry this layer to make certain I like the results, then proceed to spray more of the filter color along the sides to build up a very soft layer of dust.

○ Applying a pinwash to enhance all of the molded details on the surface of the model.

○ Filters and dust layers are built up slowly to both tint the paint and start the weathering process.

○ Stage One - the pigment application is facilitated greatly by placing the hull on its side. This makes gravity our friend when adding the dry pigments.

thoughts on the important pigment process:

• pigments are one of the best products available for us to use for the replication of earth and dirt in-scale. They have remarkable adhesion qualities and a broad allowance for applying them in different manners that create a wide range of effects from the lightest layers of dust to the thickest, wettest mud effects.

• my preference is to apply the pigments where I want them dry first, then add a liquid fixer to them, using capillary action for the pigments to absorb the liquid. I try to never touch the pigments directly with the liquid. Tamiya X-20A thinner works perfectly for this, and there are also stronger dedicated Fixers available for those thicker layered jobs.

• I apply them in this order because once dry the texture is highly accurate to real world dried earth, mud and dirt.

• After the pigments are applied and dried, I then add all sorts of dark washes to the suspension parts to recreate the various stains and wet areas present on a tank chassis.

PRO-TIP: it is best to apply large quanities of pigments with an old large wornout scruffy brush. Use a gentle tapping motion as you move the brush over the surface to spread the pigments out evenly, holding the brush about an inch above the model.

○ Stage Two - pigments are set in place with a fixing agent, such as Tamiya thinner.

○

continued thoughts on pigments:

• I prefer to mix multiple pigment colors together to recreate as much depth in the dirt as possible. Pigments are ground up paint pigments and this means they mix the same as a wet paint product. I store the mixtures in 35mm film canisters and this greatly extends the life of the pigments. Here because the Tiger chassis hides the sides of the hull so much, I only used one layer of dirt to give the impression of dried mud. Using light and dark tones would be a complete waste of time due to the somewhat limited visibility of the hull that there actually is.

• One of the most enjoyable stages is to flick stains onto the pigments and create all sorts of interesting weathering effects. Using a dark wash, I load a #2 round brush with the wash and simply flick it with the end of a flat tool to splatter the sides of the hull from a very close distance (so I don't get too much on the paint). Some stains on the paint are completely fine, and more will be added later as I now can really begin a true layering process of effects.

○ Heavy oil staining is created with dark washes applied directly onto the pigments, messy is better!

The first outer road wheel was often removed in the field to counter heavy mud buildup failures.

The heavy layer of pigments were augmented with a myriad of stains from dark washes.

thoughts on heavy weathering on suspensions:

• there is a fine balance for weathering the chassis and I tend to enjoy the visual appeal of a dirtied up lower hull, that still lets me see the mechanical aspects of the tank. Pigments really provide us the right elements to achieve this effect.

• I discovered early on that washes applied on top of pigments really give the the dirt that right amount of grimy worn look of a combat tank. However, pigments absorb a lot of liquid so my efforts are not as tidy as say the pinwash and I add gloss varnish into some of them to create a wetter look.

• New special wet effects washes are now available to help with this task, and they work great.

• Variety is the key, add big stains, small ones and many in between. But do not treat every road wheel the same, leave some almost untouched. It is the random visual effect that makes the model look more authentic, if you treat all the road wheels equally the model will look forced and artificial.

comes to adding the pigments. I lay the tracks out with the cleat side up and add the dry pigments with an old brush. Then I take an eyedropper and place large drops of thinner over the tracks until each side is soaked. I dry them with a hair dryer and flip them over and attend to the area where the road wheels run across. To give the impression of worn areas from the wheels, I used a thin sanding stick and gently rubbed it along the length of the inner faces on each side of the guide teeth. For the exposed metal, I used a more aggressive sanding stick for those areas. The result of all of this is a very realistic looking metal track that replicates the weight and sag of the real tracks quite well.

I knew that a lot more work was needed to bring this model up to the level I wanted in my head. For lack of a better word, I felt it lacked "pop" and was rather dull overall. First up was to deal with the exhaust pipes. I was far too subtle the first time around and with the help of Lifecolor's superb Rust paint set, I completely repainted and weathered both exposed pipes. I repainted each color in a thinned translucent manner letting the previous layer show thru. This added a lot of depth to the coloring and really brought it to life, as I'd hoped it would. I finished them off with Smoke from their Tensocrom paint set, and some Black Smoke pigments for the exhaust staining.

○ The finished Friul tracks after they were soaked in Blacken-it (above). The results are extraordinarily realistic, combined with pigments and washes, we have the perfect track sets.

tips for achieving success with Friulmodel tracks and Blacken-it:

• after assembly, soak the Friul tracks in a bath of kitchen vinegar for a few hours. This acts as a degreaser and preps the metal for the Blacken-it (or other similar chemical staining solutions). Rinse them off, then place them into the Blacken-it and seal the lid. I soak them for around 3-5 minutes and watch the color to see how the process is going. I shake the container every now and again to ensure even distribution. Once a nice dark brown color, I remove them.

• I dry them off completely to see the final color tones, they will lighten considerably. I then determine if I want to do a quick second bath, or move right to the pigment and washes. There will always be a few metal spots that did not get treated, these are easy to fix with paint or pigments.

thoughts on the Tiger I at this stage:

• at this point I felt I had accomplished a lot with the finish, however, after taking the model to EuroMiltaire the level of competition showed me that I had a lot left to do on this model. Upon returning home I set about to attend to a whole new level of weathering.

• it started with the dust layers, I felt they really lacked depth and were far to unbalanced from bottom to top as you moved up the model. The road wheels exhibited a heavy level of dried earth, but the rest of the model was clean by comparison.

• after this assessment, I reapplied new pigments to the road wheels and the vertical flanks of the hull, and then switched to oil paints for the upper horizontal areas of the model. This two-pronged approach dramatically changed the appearance of the project as you can see in the photos. I also bought a new Nikon DSLR camera to better capture the colors.

The new dust layers were created mainly with oil paints on the upper hull. Oils are perfect for making subtle tonal shifts in the dirt colors.

OIL PAINTS & PIGMENTS, ROUND 2

Having successfully refinished the exhaust pipes, I now turned my attention to the application of dust over the entire model. Here is where I put the most energy of any stage of this project. One of the most significant steps for effective weathering comes from the use of oil paints. I cannot think of any other product that offers up the level of control that oil paints do, as I've explained in previous chapters.

It was time for the model to really get dirty, and I wanted to give the model a proper look of use, so after the top hull plate had been re-weathered with the oils, I set about to rework the rear and the sides of the hull next. I used a lightened batch of the first pigments that I made and for the rear hull, set the model carefully on its nose and replicated the heavy pigment application that I previously used on the lower hull sides. I was a bit more random with how I placed the pigments here and that is what led to the rather patchy appearance of the final result.

The sides however were much trickier and required a lot more care to get just right. Because I already had a base of dust layering to start from, I chose to use oils first. I started by adding thin layers of Abt. 093 Basic Earth along the lower edge of the sides. I followed this with a light layer of pigments that were then set with Fixer via the airbrush, which adds a very subtle softness and discoloration over the oils. Now here is the tricky part: I then took a clean flat rake-style brush that has a super fine edge and with some Fixer dragged the brush down the sides in a vertical motion. After that, I sprinkled the pigments as you see here--concentrated around the rear corner area and then very gently airbrushed more Fixer on top. To finish it off, I then took the same rake brush and gently repeated the vertical streaking, and was very careful to not remove too much of the pigment clumps on the side as possible.

With the hull sides and rear up to par and looking like what I was ultimately after, the front end required some extra effort too. However, on the front, I was not looking for the same gritty texture that I created on the lower sides and rear. I wanted the front to have a heavier, yet finer layer of dust. To do this, I aggressively scrubbed in the pigments dry and then sprayed Fixer over this. I repeated the layering process a few more times to build a higher level of opacity with the end result being a more consistent and dusty appearance. To finish it off, I used

Stage One - the light rust tones are applied first in very thin layers to preserve transparency.

Stage Two - continue with the next darker rust shade, again heavily thinned to slowly build up the opacity.

Stage Three - the darkest color is applied last and concetrated on the lower half of the exhaust pipes.

Stage Four - the exhausts are completed with some Tensocrom Smoke and Black Smoke pigments.

tips for applying pigments to vertical hull sides:

• the trickiest aspect to applying pigments is to a vertical exposed surface. To help, create a stable setup whereby you can stand the model on end to work on the section you want in a horizontal fashion. Make gravity your friend, don't fight it.

• the first pigment layer should set the tone of the dirt color and how heavy the application will be. For example, I wanted a lot more pigments on the rear hull than along the sides above the tracks. My first layer on the rear (seen below) was rather opaque and covered most of the back plate.

• after the first layer is dried, then you can begin to build up deeper areas as you like. By altering the pigment color (usually lighter tones on top) you can increase the visual depth dramatically for a very authentic look. Remember between each dry application is a quick application of the fixing liquid. You can work wet or dry by adding more pigments on top while it is still wet to build up more unique effects.

• for the final details like dirt splatters or spotty appearance, hold the pigment application brush farther away from the surface so they disperse more randomly as they hit the model. You can see the results of this on the upper half of the rear hull below.

the same rake-style brush and added some subtle vertical streaking with Fixer to create a harmonious look with the pigments over the model sides.

I then decided the outer road wheels needed additional effects to bring them up to the same levels that the rest of the model now showed. Here I went back to using the oil paints to add in the same richer earth tones that I had applied above. I have no qualms with layering oils over pigments, and in fact think some of the resulting effects can be very unique and realistic. In this case, a bit more thinner was used since the pigments tend to absorb any extra liquid.

Time was now spent on the turret, and even though it was a smaller amount of surface area to deal with than the hull, the extra weathering still required a fair amount of time to complete. Fundamentally, I repeated all of the same steps that I used earlier with the hull, but I used lighter versions of the colors to keep the model properly balanced. It is usually a more realistic look to apply lighter colors the higher up the model you go. This adds to the visual weight of the piece and your eyes read the model in a correct manner with the darker heavier areas down low. I also used less quanitities for the obvious reason that it is a lot harder for large amounts of dust and dirt to get up on the top surfa-

○ By dropping more dry pigments onto the wet lower layer underneath I was able to create this unique texture.

○ The wheels were fully attended to whether they would be visible or not. Here the inner faces are all treated to unique stains.

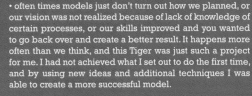

○

thoughts on applying another round of weathering:

• often times models just don't turn out how we planned, or our vision was not realized because of lack of knowledge of certain processes, or our skills improved and you wanted to go back over and create a better result. It happens more often than we think, and this Tiger was just such a project for me. I had not achieved what I set out to do the first time, and by using new ideas and additional techniques I was able to create a more successful model.

• this project was the one that really got me to use oil paints in a serious manner. I learned after doing extensive dust layers with them that oils were very powerful and had a lot of potential uses. This eventually led to my concept of Oil Paint Rendering. Progress in modeling requires moments of reflection and to ask ourselves "what more can I do?", or "that new idea would really be perfect for my project." You can often move to the next step by doing so.

ces. Plus, that is where the crew moves around the most, which in turn will keep the area freer from dust and dirt.

NEARING THE END

I was finally coming to the end of the long process of reworking the entire weathering on this model, but a few areas still needed more work. These included areas like the hull top section adjacent to the front engine intake grilles on either side of the turret race, which required another round of oils and pigments to get better depth to the dust colors. I added more contrast, and as a result made the center engine access panel stand out more thru variations in contrast and/or opacity. After I corrected this area, I continued to go around the entire model and tweaked each spot to ensure everything had a pleasing balance and contrast to the surrounding areas. Hopefully my vigilance paid off, because the final element to add was the myriad of stains that gives the model that last touch of looking like a true combat veteran. Once the stains were applied that would basically conclude the weathering processes, so

○ On the outer road wheels, I went back over the original pigments with a whole new layer, inlcuding new stains.

layers, layers, and even more layers: ○

• during the course of weathering the second time around, the ever powerful idea of layers really came to the forefront of my process. If you study areas like the road wheels carefully, you can see pigments, stains, more pigments, more stains and so on. By varying some layers between different wheels I was able to achieve subtlely different looks between them. This is all a result of layers. And each layer does not have to maintain the same verve as the previous layer, there is no hard rule to follow, simply use the layering concept and the processes involved to create the final look.

89

tips on using oil paints for dust layers:

• as previously mentioned, switching to oils for the new dust on the upper hull was key to realizing the look I wanted to achieve. I combined them with layers of dust pigments to arrive at the final results seen through the rest of this chapter.

• I chose three shades of earth and light dirt color oils, and after making a simple cardboard palette, I applied the oils in the same manner as I discuss and illustrate in the earlier OPR chapter. I place the color I want, where I want, then blend it out with a clean brush nearly dry of thinner on it. I used the darker tones to replicate a wetter or fresher dirt area, and the lighter colors are used to show a drier thinner layer of dust.

• keep the effects random, yet believable. Use the joints and corners of the model as collection points for the dust because this is how it happens in the real world.

I wanted to make sure I had everything completed to the right levels beforehand.

To recreate the stains, I first made a dark almost black wash mixture that was a bit thicker than normal. This would be used to reproduce oil and grease stains in general. I also made a lighter dark brown mixture that I used in conjunction with the near black one to provide a bit of variety with the stains. These would dry much lighter and thus look older and less intense. I layered this with the washes to replicate the dirt, oil, fuel and general grime on the rear deck. When doing this step, I tend to take a bit more artistic license with the stains in an effort to create an original and unique vehicle. Sometimes you can push

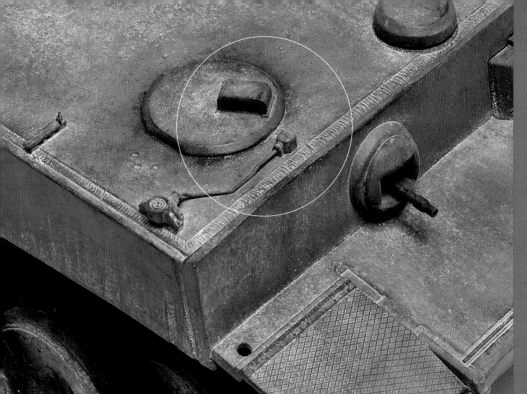

○

tips for using pigments and oil paints together for dust effects:

• this layered product idea was a real exciting process because it gave me the best of both worlds. I achieved a gritty dusty look from the pigments, and was able to have darker tones and streaked dust effects with the oils.

• to recreate a gritty thin dust layer the paint surface must be matte. Using a small amount of light colored pigments on the scruffy brush, carefully apply it to the model and scrub it in realistic patterns around the details. Then with some fixer loaded in an airbrush, very very gently mist the fixer across the surface (maybe as low as 8psi) holding the airbrush a good 6" away from the model. You do not want to blow away all the pigments, instead you want the light mist of fixer to rain down and capture it on the surface. It takes a few practice runs on scrap to get the feel for it, but it works perfectly for thin dust layers and will even hold up well because the liquid fixer wets the pigments just enough to set them in place. I also use a variety of smaller pigment brush sizes to get into smaller areas too.

• from here you can integrate oil paint effects around and on top of the dust pigments, in the same manner as before.

○ Combinations of dark oils and the dust pigments are used to create a worn hatch area. Note the clean surroundings from the crew.

○ The rear engine deck is treated to a myriad of oil stains, layered on top of dust pigments, and then the final dark stains are added around the edges of the large hatch opening.

○ The model is now nearing completion, with the extra efforts to rework the weathering paying off nicely.

○

thoughts for striking a balance between heavy weathering and believability:

• this is one of the more contested concepts and a constantly moving target born of new techniques and ideas to push our models even farther. I am usually a fan of heavy weathering, but I am always trying to maximize my efforts to keep it all *in-scale*. Out-of-scale effects are a greater cause for concern than the actual quanity of the weathering applied.

• believability comes directly from studying reference of all sorts. Without it, we have no guage to relate these things to, and there are a lot of dirty muddy chipped and scratched vehicles around to get a greater sense of how things look, beyond general armor photos. Use as much reference resources as necessary to create the final results.

summary of thoughts to this point of the weathering process:

• layering is fundamental to the end result. Layering of processes, techniques and products all work together to create the subtle and not so subtle effects. Look carefully above at the different stains and you can begin to discern old ones, newer ones--the oil paints and pigments all working in concert together. It doesn't happen all at once, both in real life and during the weathering. Build them up over time using a wide range of opacities.

• choose weathering colors complimetary to the vehicle colors within a range of historically accurate tones applicable to the geography and season the model is presented in. For example, summer dirt looks different to winter dirt within the same region due to difference in temperature and moisture content.

• do not be afraid to rework a process, or an entire model if you are not satisfied. Self-improvement is a critical element for scale modeling over time. This will help with confidence and being able to realize your end goals on a project. I learned an enormous amount during the second round of weathering on this one and am thankful I took it upon myself to rework the finish.

• studying reference of all sorts will really help build up a library of knowledge on what looks correct and authentic.

one realm further than the other, and this is such a case with the final weathering elements. To me it is almost like adding your signature, and as such is like saying this is my model and what I'm about. It is what gives the model that needed bit of life. I learned this back when I was studying design in school and producing detailed renderings for my work. I found it was always that last 5% of the messing around with the drawing that really allowed it to reach its full potential. I use the same principles here.

I used the same basic flicking of the brush idea on the rest of the model too. You can also execute this same basic idea with a pigment/wash mixture. Just remember that the pigments will dry much lighter than the color of when they are wet, but it is a perfect method to replicate mud splatters from a vehicle driving quickly off-road. Some people have even taken this idea further and used their airbrush to blow a wet pigment mixture over the rear areas of a model to replicate generous amounts of splattered mud. Either way, control is the best approach and I recommend building up the effect slowly, checking your progress often to see how it is turning out. You can always add more, but never take it away, so proceed with caution when doing this final stage. I would hate for someone to get all the way to the end and then ruin their model using this method.

FROM START TO FINISH

My thoughts turn back to the start of this project and how impressive the kit was at its introduction. We naysayers stood in disbelief at how far Dragon had come in such a short time frame. Those feelings were helped by the fact that no one was expecting it, so surprise was on their side. Of course, since then we have been witness to a relentless release schedule of associated German WWII armor kits in 1/35. Most of them are superior to what has come before it and have really set the standard.

thoughts on pushing through tough spots to get to the end result:

• it must be remembered that quality work takes time and practice to arrive at the final completion stage. This project lasted nearly 3 years of on and off again work. While this is certainly not normal, it can definitely happen when a model stalls out. Lack of motivation, inspiration, reference, or a busy schedule can all interfere and cause delays. For this model, I hit a plateau and then I found new inspiration from other modeler's work and this sparked new efforts. This day of the Internet provides us with so much access to a fantastic amount of material and other modeler's projects, we are very lucky in this regards. I hope the models in these pages can do the same for one, or more of you, as well.

○ Creating a unique area of interest does not always need to be from stowage or figures, it can come from a totally unexpected weathering effect.

○

tips for creating unique one-off special effects:

• because Tigers are rarely seen loaded down with extra gear, and I did not add a figure I had a desire to add a special effect for a cool focal point to the finish. I chose to add a large wet stain on the front armor down low forcing the viewer in to further study the model's finish.

• I did this because I felt I had created a very nice dust layer on the front hull, but rarely is this area looked at, especially down low. I great solution to draw the viewer in to enjoy this area was the wet stain. I used dark brown oil paint thinned down a little bit, then I simply proceeded to paint the stain on top of the dust pigment layer. This resulted in the color staying dark after it dried giving the impression of a large wet area or oil stain in the surface.

• the rear engine deck was given a very similar treatment with black and dark brown oil paint stains as well, and a special fuel stain was added with Lifecolor's unique Tensocrom Fuel effect paint.

thoughts on asymmetrical weathering:

• I often study my model in-progress to ensure that I am not creating overly symmetrical weathering effects. I find it much more natural and visually pleasing to have a fair amount of asymmetry within the weathering finish. The hatch on the right has a different quantity of wear to the one on the left, the right fender is dusted to a different opacity level than the left one, stains are extremely random and often concentrated in various areas to achieve a more realistic appearance. I know it can be a cliche, but I really try to contain certain weathering aspects to what I perceive as areas of heavy crew usage. Their uniforms can act like a cleaning rag when they sit on the turrets edge taking a break, or halfway outside a hatch opening, so it will have less dust present as a result.

Sd.Kfz 181

The Tiger I represents one of the pinnacle combat tanks of WWII, and as such it carries a tremendous amount of mystique and legend with it. Its strength and power were undeniable and the brutal squat look of it with its mighty "Eighty-Eight" reaching out only lend credence to this notion. By producing this kit, Dragon "re-entered" the 1/35 armor model market in a big way and the results are nothing short of exceptional. Additional releases in this series have maintained its impressive quality and accuracy.

I think this aspect gave my project a lot of extra weight and I personally wanted to achieve a level of finish with it that matched the character of the vehicle itself. So many amazing Tiger I models have been made in years past, however, when I began this project my skills were not as good as when I completed it. The process was long, I learned so much along the way and I had to source new ideas and sought new inspiration to truly arrive at a satisfactory result.

This model represents a true transitional modeling period of time for me and this makes it even more special in that regards. During its long gestation timeframe, I developed the concepts of layering, using oil paints, and combining multiple products and techniques together to achieve certain effects. I consider this model one of those plateau breaking builds that pushed me to the next level with my skills and I look back at it in fondness because of this. These thoughts also reside on top of the significance of modeling an Initial Tiger I, (my very first Tiger project, in fact), and pushing a Panzer-grau paintjob to its fullest. It truly redefined my work.

PANZERKAMPFWAGEN

Pz Kpfw Tiger mit 8.8cm KwK36 L/56

VI TIGER INITIAL PROD

1 BASE COAT

2 FIRST CAMO LAYER

3 MARKINGS

4 SECOND CAMO LAYER

5 DETAIL PAINTING

6 CHIPPING WITH THINNER

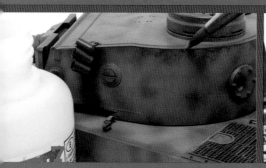

7 CHIPPING WITH THINNER

8 PAINTING CENTER OF CHIPS

9 APPLY TURRET NUMBERS

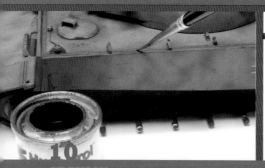

10 PINWASH

11 FILTER

12 PIGMENTS - APPLY DRY

13 PIGMENTS - FIXER

14 PIGMENTS - STAINS

15 PIGMENTS - ROAD WHEELS

16 MOUNT ROAD WHEELS

17 FINAL ROAD WHEEL DETAILS

18 FRIUL ASSEMBLY - BLACKEN IT™

19 TRACKS COMPLETED

20 TRACKS MOUNTED

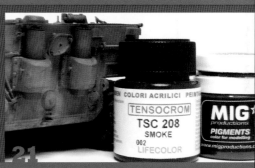

21 EXHAUSTS REPAINTED

22 OIL PAINT RENDERING

23 PIGMENTS REDONE

24 FINAL PIGMENTS & OPR DUST

JAGDPANZER 38(t) für

Jgd Pz 38(t) Hetzer für 7.5cm PaK39 L/48

Gerät 555

The Jagdpanzer 38(t) Hetzer model from Tamiya may well be my favorite kit to build. And that goes for each scale that they make it in -- 1/35 and 1/48. Having built one of each previously, both Hetzer kits are simply gems of injection molded scale model engineering. In the same manner the Dragon Tiger I series mimics the intense complexity of the real tank in kit form with its myriad of parts and sub-assemblies, the Tamiya Hetzer stands in stark contrast, and defines the mantra of simplicity for both design and kit construction, again in the same manner that the real vehicle was created to achieve. It was a design good enough to serve the Swiss Army in the post-war era, and was a very clever adaptation of a tank design that was created before the war started.

When it comes to paint schemes, the Hetzer also provides us with a surprising element of contrast to its simple efficient design engineering with some of the most complex camo schemes employed during the war. The most unique of which are referred to as "ambush schemes", and these were factory applied camo patterns that followed strict principles in German camoflage theory that provide us with very interesting patterns to replicate. And let's not overlook the fact that this particular scheme is also hard-edged by nature, and this will require extra efforts and planning to replicate fully.

The duality of this subject makes for a very interesting and unique project, whereby the smooth easy going and enjoyable build is bookended with a tightly formed intricate paint job that requires a smart and well-planned approach, and when broken down into acheiavable steps becomes a far simpler task. Creating an accurate ambush scheme model is something that provides true rewards.

7.5cm PaK39 HETZER

EASE OF CONSTRUCTION

One of the shortest conversations that we as armor modelers could have would be to discuss the construction of the Tamiya Hetzer kit. I could easily sum it as open the box, clip the parts off, remove the burrs and sand off seam lines, and then simply read the instruction and follow the steps until completed, it will take only a few hours. It really is that good of a kit, from both an accuracy point and a fitment perspective. As the cliche goes, no kit is perfect, but Tamiya has done a very admirable job of providing us with a state-of-the-art kit that captures the look of the subject faithfully and goes together like a great model should, allowing us to spend time on all the other aspects worth noting, such as super-detailing or the finish. If ever there was a prime candidate for a high-quality out-of-the-box kit to simply glue together and enjoy the paintjob and know the final results are pretty damn accurate, this kit is on the Top 10 list of models for sure.

And such was the nature of this project -- enjoy the build, and then put maximum effort into the painting and weathering, and in this case, tackle the challenge of replicating a factory hard-edge ambush scheme in all its glory. But first, it is necessary to build the model and as indicated by my comments so far, it is a joy to assemble. Thoughtful touches abound, and in recent Tamiya fashion they ensure as mistake free of a build as possible. The suspension bogies for example are set in exact height by a very handy sprue part that keeps all level while the glue dries.

Taking a cue from their successful line of 1/48 kits, Tamiya provide the tracks as superbly cast link-and-length plastic pieces that actually fit perfectly together allowing for the correct amount of track sag to be imparted into them as they dry, all of which really helps the ease of assembly. While I was admittedly very tempted to swap in a set of Friuls (when am I not?),

○ Overall view of the completed Hetzer, it was an exercise in replicating one of the most complicated camo patterns used in WWII.

thoughts on proper planning to achieve the goals of the project:

• within each project lies the heart of the exercise, in this case it was the ambush scheme camoflage. Never an easy thing to recreate, it takes research and quality reference to be able lay out the process that is best utilized to see it realized successfully. On top of which, it takes further internalizing to understand the best way to weather such a scheme that still captures the look and feeling of it, without ruining the effects. The hard-edge 3-color pattern has such unique visual appeal that whatever weathering is applied should be mindful of those efforts so you have a balanced and sound piece of modeling once complete.

• not every model needs to have every new technique or weathering product applied to it, and in the case of this Jagdpazner, the camo is extremely busy and intricate already, so the weathering was kept to some fundamental and effective methods only.

○ Completion of the basic assembly is rapid, fit and finish are exemplary and the details excellent overall. Thinning the fenders was about the only modifications made.

○ The tracks and road wheels were glued together as unit for ease of painting later on.

these tracks were too good to not give them a try and see how well they can be painted to represnt the level of finish I wanted to achive with them.

The rest of the model is rather straightforward assembly, with everything literally falling in to place. Even the main gun barrel is used from the kit, it is that nice and true. My efforts, therefore, were concentrated on thinning certain parts to better represent scale thickness, and that means on any Hetzer kit thinning the front and rear fenders. Sure there are wonderful PE sets for this purpose, so you have options either way. But sticking to the OOB theme, I loved using what is given and receive satisfaction working in such a manner of this time-honored tradition. I also dirlled out the two small antenna holder brackets on the left side of the hull, and since I was drilling holes, I opened up the end of the muffler to make it look like real exhaust tubing, which is always thin-walled steel piping.

thoughts on enjoying some quality out-of-the-box modeling: ◯

• kits that provide us with superb construction and accuracy like this one deserve some good OOB modeling efforts from time to time. Not that the model wouldn't look excellent with a full PE suite applied, but it is just as rewarding sometimes to relax, open the box and begin construction sans worrying about recreating a super-detailed project. Tamiya provides all we need to truly realize a superb Hetzer on the sprues, and that was one less thing to worry about because this project was really more about the ambush scheme than anything else. I'll save the extra construction efforts for the next time I build one.

◯ Track sag is acheived by gently bending the top runs of the tracks and glueing them to the return roller to hold them in place.

JAGDPANZER 38(t) HETZER

paint callouts for the Panther project:

• **GREEN CAMO:** I try to choose colors slightly lighter in tone than I want the end result to be. For the green I found *Lifecolor UA132 Light Green RLM 83* a great out of the bottle choice here.

• **GREY PRIMER:** A great choice in most cases for a grey primer barrel is *Tamiya XF-24 Dark Grey* mixed with a few drops *XF-69 NATO Gray*, plus a drop of *XF-7 Flat Red*.

• **DUNKELGELB:** Hetzer photos in ambush schemes show the Dunkelgelb to be quite light, nearly white sometimes so I chose *Lifecolor UA090 Sand* as my starting point.

• **RED BROWN:** This color is always a bit tricky with late-war paint schemes. It is easy to confuse true red brown with red primer in the final days of the war, so I went *Lifecolor UA088 Italian Mimetic Brown 2* for this choice because it struck the right balance.

quick ref:

• **CAMO GREEN:**
UA132 Light Green
RLM83

• **RED BROWN:**
UA088 Italian Mimetic
Brown 2

• **DUNKELGELB:**
UA090 Sand

• **GREY PRIMER:**
XF-24 Dark Grey
XF-69 NATO Gray
XF-7 Flat Red

BASE COLORS

Getting started with the paintjob is really where some proper thought and planning are necessary given the challenge of creating a high-quality and accurate ambush camoflage scheme. At the time of this project, there were no masks on the market to facilitate the task, so that meant only one viable option was available -- handmade masks. And for this process there is really only one decent choice to use for masks and that is using Tamiya yellow tape, a truly fantastic product that I always keep in stock. It adheres well to the surface, lays down tight for a clean edge, and has a low tack backing that won't damage the paint underneath. Because of the precision of the camo pattern required, I would not recommend using Silly Putty or similar moldable clay type products (Blu-tac) for this type of pattern masking. These factory applied schemes used repetitive hard masks and followed set patterns.

But before I get to the masks, I had to decide on the first

TANKART
108

tips for prepping and painting base colors :

• airbrushing the first colors is always best to spray in thin layers, then build up the opacity slowly. Never try to get the color down in one go. The distance of the tip of the airbrush to the model is usually around 3-4", kept perpendicular to the section, and move your hand in a steady pattern, not lingering in any one spot too long to avoid excess build up.

• for the clean separation of the two base colors shown below, I used tape along the underside of the sponson for a simple mask.

• LC paints lay down best slightly wet because they settle and dry very tight to the surface. If it hits too dry it will pebble slightly leaving a rough texture to the paint.

○ Stage One - primer layer via my favorite choice - Mr. Surfacer 1200.

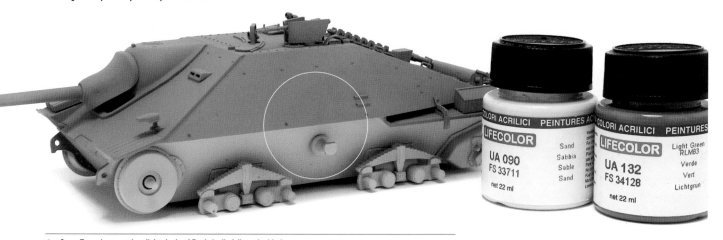

○ Stage Two - basecoat in a light shade of Dunkelgelb, followed with the green camo on top.

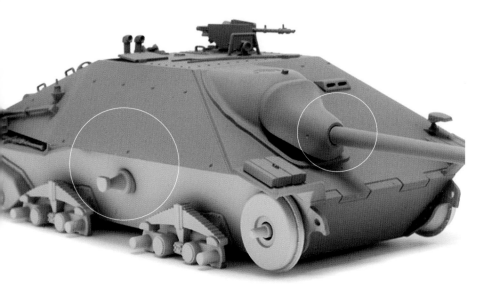

○ The resulting colors are light in tone and ready for the all important ambush scheme coming next.

color layer, which I would add the ambush pattern on top of. My choice was simple, paint the basecoat of the model in the dominant color, then add the other two colors over this. On this vehicle, the green is the most prominant, and that is what I painted first on the upper hull. Of course, I primed the bare plastic beforehand with my favorite Mr. Surfacer 1200 primer. After that I laid down a light Sand from Lifecolor to represent the lighter tone of Dunkelgelb used on these Panzerjagers on the lower chassis areas, which aren't camouflaged. Now I was ready to spray the green upper hull and I used another Lifecolor paint, a aircraft color RLM83 Light Green actually, because I liked the tone and I always start with a lighter than required camo color since the weathering will build up darker tones from this point onward. Otherwise the end result would be a very dark and out-of-scale looking model. As you read this book series, you will see I prefer starting with lighter base colors on nearly every project due to this darkening issue within the weathering processes.

JAGDPANZER 38(t) HETZER

tips for replicating the intricate ambush scheme with Tamiya tape masks:

• it all starts with having plans of the ambush scheme, and Tamiya provides this in the kit via a full-color illustration page. However, you cannot simply scale the plans to 1/35 and trace them because the armor is all sloped and this distorts the pattern in side, top and end views. Only the very top flat panel is true to scale in plan view. So you must hand drawt them.

• I began with drawing the yellow areas first, then cutting each individual piece out to apply and spray it one at a time. This kept mistakes and overspray to an absolute minimum. I moved onto the red brown next, then the small shadow flakes as the last layer applied.

• any mistakes or soft edges were carefully hand painted afterwards.

○ All of the factory applied schemes followed templated patterns applied the same way.

MASKING

It's no surprise that the most important part of the painting for this project is replicating the detailed camo pattern, and thankfully Tamiya provides a full color sheet clearly illustrating the pattern on the entire Hetzer. This was a huge help even though I had great reference photos from the Ground Power Japanese reference book on the Jagdpanzer 38(t), which is old and long out of print. As mentioned earlier, the pattern is factory applied with masks, and the best method I found was to simply draw the pattern of each hard-edge cloud shape onto the Tamiya tape, cut it out with a fresh hobby knife, lay the mask on the model and spray the color. This worked very well and I repeated the task for all the light tan spot, and then the dark red brown areas. For the small shadow flecks, I made a series of masks that included bunches of the small shapes cut out and I mix and matched them until the model was properly coverded with them, studying the ref. in detail to try to capture the scale and quantity properly. I also properly painted the side skirts during this process as well, even though I don't show them in the photos until later after they were added on.

This masking and painting procedure was no easy task, but because I broke it down into manageable steps, it went off without a hitch. The Tamiya tape performed precisely as intended and the results were quite accurate, taking everything into account. I do believe there are now aftermarket ambush camo masks that are available, and I'm sure these would go even further to facilitating the tedious task of painting this sort of pattern.

○ The shadow flakes were applied last and with multiple pattern masks to provide a greater variety of shapes.

thoughts on the painting results so far:

• I find it very helpful to review my work at important stages. Up to this point, the effort was focused on the ambush pattern and trying to make it accurate as possible. A lot of effort was spent studying the photos and drawings of this scheme, and I felt it hinged on the size and quantity of the smaller shadow flakes most of all. I've seen other modelers make these too large and has a bad affect on the look of this pattern. I'm happy the results of the work so far in this regards, the research really paid off.

• Now I had to switch gears and think about the weatherin again, I had a good idea already in my head that I didn't want to do any winter weathering and was looking for a dirty well-used vehicle, but not overly combat tortured. These light Jagdpanzers were effectively hit-and-run units by design so I kept my focus on subtle wear and tear for this project.

• I used the details like the tools and exhaust to further break up the visual effects of the camoflage. It does its job very well and the model sort of disappears after painting, so I painted the tools, gun barrel and accessories in strong contrasting colors to bring some balance back to the overall look of the model.

○ Tricky areas like the tool box requiered more than one mask, plus some hand painting to complete.

JAGDPANZER 38(t) HETZER

○ To further break up the effective camoflage I painted the markings and details in strong contrasting colors.

○ Reference photos showed Hetzer barrels painted in grey primer were common from the factory.

○

tips for completing the detail painting in a hassle free manner:

• typically when painting armor, you can airbrush the entire built model as one unit, and then go back and attend to the smaller details like the tools, exhausts, barrels and so on. In this case, I broke the model down into the hull and track/road wheel assembly to facilitate the process, and if this was a tank, the turret would painted separately too.

• to paint all the small items it is best to use a good brush painting acrylic like Lifecolor or Vallejo and thin it a little more and use good quality brushes. Protect the model underneath each tool with small pieces of paper as you go and the process should be clean and straightforward.

• use the small details to help visually improve the model and don't skimp on this process, these areas should receive as much attention as the rest of the model and can really set it apart in the end. I'm a fan and believer of models that showcase such attention to detail, they can really go far to help elevate a project to the next level.

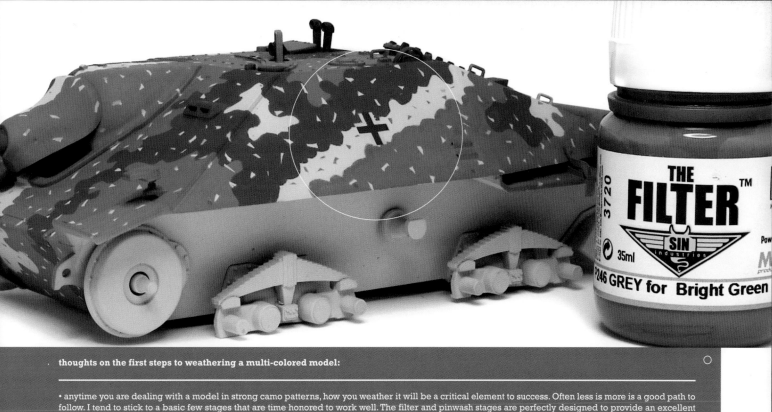

thoughts on the first steps to weathering a multi-colored model:

• anytime you are dealing with a model in strong camo patterns, how you weather it will be a critical element to success. Often less is more is a good path to follow. I tend to stick to a basic few stages that are time honored to work well. The filter and pinwash stages are perfectly designed to provide an excellent starting point. To avoid issues, work with the lightest color in the pattern to ensure this colors stay true. The grey-tan filter color above works well and colors within this range of tones overall are good to work with for filters, whether they are self-made or aftermarket products.

○ The pinwash is perfect to bring back the detail, including adding initial stains and streaks.

tips for achieving success with the pinwash:

• one of the most important steps in my modeling is the pinwash. I use it in lieu of other techniques namely pre- and post-shading. I also give full credit to Mario Eens for showing me the insight to use a pinwash for the first level of weathering. The intentions are to bring out the details molded on the surface and I much prefer the precision and control afforded by this process.

• use of a fine tipped brush is a key element to achieving success because you want to place the pinwash exactly onto each detail and not in an overall general wash style fashion. This works to keep the base colors intact and lend the model soft shadows on these details that remain in scale, plus you have already applied a filter so another wash layer isn't necessary.

• while doing this step, take advantage of the fact that while adding the pinwash early on in the weathering you can also begin to add other subtle effects as you work because you already have the proper enamel wash in hand to do it, such as dirt streaks and minor staining. In the same manner as in OPR, I use a series of clean blending brushes to work with the pinwash as seen below. I use them to create the host of subtle streaks and to blend any errant tidemarks that may arise after the wash has dried a bit.

Working with the pinwash over the entire model achieves the first level of weathering and helps guide the next steps.

As each area of the pinwash is applied, I work efficiently to add streaks and stains at the same time. I find by doing this I get a great idea how the model will turn out in the end.

WEATHERING BEGINS

With the camo paintjob completed, the model is ready to get marked up. Crosses were spray masked on using Eduard's easy system, and the tools and small fittings were all hand painted in their appropriate colors. Next is the filter, which on this model really helped to tone the colors down and harmonize the look of the model. This sets the stage for the pinwashes.

One note to make is with the road wheels and tracks. A great construction technique for such styles of running gear is to assemble the tracks and wheels as a unit that can then simply slide onto the stub axles. The point is to faciliate painting both sides and I did this in the previous step. So with that task done, I was able to weather them during the same processes discribed below.

Pinwashes were perfect for bringing back some definition to the camo'd Hezter because the ambush pattern is very effective and the details immediately get lost in the painting. Because of this, I went with a stronger color to the pinwash to add visual strength to this step, and working with both MIG Dark and Brown washes, I went over the entire model using a #2 Round tip application brush.

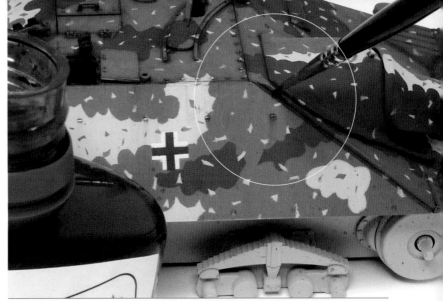

○ Using various colors on this camo scheme helps to reinforce the details such as the main panel lines.

○

thoughts on weathering the early stages:

• I talk about it often, and the reality is the early weathering stages are often some of the most fundamental steps to a successful end result. I say this because if you attempt to arrive at the end result in a blunt manner, the completed model will show this. Having these early subtle layers are what gives you the ability to have layers to begin with, so avoid the temptation to lay down the final colors right away.

• I do things this way because it also prevents disasters from happening and keeps the processes in check. It can be extremely frustrating to get so far into a project to only have something go wrong by overdoing it early on. Mistakes can always happen, of course, but this mental and physical pace mitigates the potential negative possibilities, which is a great way to stay happy with the progress of the model.

○ The dirt and dust layers are the next steps after the pinwash. I work on the model in two separate stages, the tracks and road wheel assembly as one stage, then the hull was weathered to match.

○ **thoughts on achieving the dust and dirt tones to illustrate the goals of the project:**

• I know from the conversations I've had with fellow modelers that choosing the right dirt and earth colors can be challenging. You arrive at this stage ready to get the model dirty, but that hesitation from picking out the right colors is not all that uncommon. When I choose pigment colors I don't just pick one. I start by choosing the season to determine the moisture levels that should be present, this also tells me how much dust is needed in relation to the dried mud. I then go by the model's tones. Here the paintjob is somewhat cool overall with a hint of warm tones in the red brown, but not too much. From this analysis, I pick out 4-5 pigments (sometimes more) and this will be my base range of colors that I mix together for the model. The colors are neutral tans and some light greyish tans. I stay away from the reds and dark mud colors. After mixing and applying, the blended pigments dry with a lot of depth and visual interest. The colors compliment the model and look believable. Only known regional earth colors are pre-determined, such Vietnam earth, which is very red in color. If the model was a lot warmer in one I would use more light browns, yellowish tans, and so forth.

○ Hand painting chips and scratches requires a fine tipped brush and thinned paint to apply the marks in a natural fashion.

tips for achieving such with hand painted chips and scratches:

• not every model requires HS chipping, as much as I do love the technique. We often have models that can work equally well using more traditional methods such as brush painting and using small pieces of sponges. If the model doesn't require a lot of surface effects, these two tools are great for this task.

• I always use thinned paints when chipping, this is important because the chips are being painted *on top* of the paintjob, so thick paint will look very fake right away. Thinned paint dries much tighter and level with the rest of the paint, giving us the proper impression of distressed wear and tear.

• apply the marks in a sensible fashion, along the vehicle's exposed spots that would commonly encountered other objects, such as the side skirts. I use them to good affect to showcase this idea. It also helps to use good vision equipment to get really close to the model to create as small as marks as you can.

○ I used a combination of a sponge and a brush to create these marks. To create long steady horizontal marks run your hand or brush along a bridge to steady your movement.

thoughts on painting exhausts:

• painting exhausts are always going to be important elements when they are prominently displayed on the outside of the vehicle. Because of their propensity to rust and quickly look worn out, these are perfect targets for us to give them extra weathering attention. The basic idea is to apply rust tones in a manner that has a lot of visual texture within the colors, not simply painting it one single rust color. Rust ranges in tones from yellows to dark browns and this is an important effect to capture in the exhaust pipes.

• In truth any quality paints would work even though I use the Lifecolor Rust paints a lot. There are also new similar products coming to market, but you are free to choose similar colors from your bench if you want to use those instead. And the principles are exactly the same, thin the paints first and apply them in translucent layering applications to build up the paint's opacities. This creates the tonal variety you see below.

• it is often more visually interesting to maintain some of the base paints into the exhaust painting. Most of the paint would likely burn off in short order, but some would possibly remain intact, creating this effect, which also illustrated below.

PIGMENTS

Once the pinwashes are dried and completed, including some initial stains and streaks for good measure, the first round of pigments are applied next. I add a mixture of dry pigments to the hull in the same manner as described in the Tiger I chapter -- by placing the hull on its side and then covering the side with dry pigments, add the fixer to set them in place, dry it all off, then add a myriad of dark wash stains. I also treat the tracks, plus the inner and outer surfaces of the large road wheels with the same pigments and washes, and mount the two subassemblies to the model. To finishing the wheels, I add dark stains to show lubrication maintenance and oil leaks around the center hubs.

CHIPPING

With the details all painted, the filter, pinwashes, and

○ Stages One & Two - I add the rust tones directly over the painted exhaust, starting with the lightest color first, then working in the next color while it's still wet to create the above visual effects.

○ Stage Three - I continue to build up the rust tones with darker colors, keeping the layers thin and transparent to build the opacity.

○ Stage Four - the final dark rust tones give it the depth to look authentic, and the tip is topped off with some black discoloration.

the first round of pigments applied, I then attended to the main chipping of the model. Unlike my newer models using the Hairspray technique, for this project I stuck with more traditional chipping methods, namely a brush and a steady hand. I used a simple two color process and hand painted dark colored chips and scratches by hand with thinned acrylic colors. Once I finished that task, I carefully highlighted the lower edge of some of the larger chips to give them a 3D look, which is clearly seen on the front of the side skirts. The rest of the model had very subtle chips and scratches only, as I'm always trying to keep such effects in-scale, regardless of the technique used.

EXHAUSTS

So far in each of the armor subjects within this book, the exhausts have come in for some added attention. Many German tank designs used exposed exhaust systems, so this makes perfect sense and in truth, I love it. I really do enjoy painting rusty exhausts and this one was no different. Like the Tiger I model, I used the incredible Lifecolor Rust & Dust paint set to its fullest. The ability to layer up the rust tones in a translucent manner make them extremely effective tools for the task. If you study or look at old automobile exhausts, you will note that it takes years to develop a really pitted texture, so

○ For the righthand side skirts, I intentionally weathered them a lot more subtlely than the other side to reinforce the reasons why I muddied the left side, which was a result of driving through wet mud.

○ **tips for achieving balance and visual interest with the weathering effects:**

• weathering is so much more than simply the process of making a vehicle look worn and dirty. Weathering is the main element that tells the viewer the story of the vehicle and how we present this is a defining characteristic that must be embraced to its fullest. On this model, I used the dirt effects to the maximum to illustrate the previous movements of the Hetzer.

• I also worked the weathering to control the viewer's eye movement and tried to incorporate some interesting effects that could be further appreciated as a result. Areas like the left front fender and the heavy mud splashes I added, or the rear hull plate literally covered completely in dirt, and then the subtle rain streaks on the right hand side skirts that stand in contrast to the left. And so on, all the while continually monitoring my process to manage this concept throughout the weathering stages.

○

tips for moving to the next stages in the weathering process:

• at this point in the finish, it is time to fade the paint more, add additional and stronger streaks and stains in the paint, and in general increase the level of wear and tear. Per my normal, I turn to oil paints to create these effects. Using OPR, I go over each section of the model and address the paint tones, apply dirty areas from the crew, add more rust and dirt streaks, rain streaks in the dust, and fade certain panels to break up the model a little bit more. This is easily acheive with the oils, and they work perfectly for this concept. I also work with a lot of lighter tones to keep the model from getting too dark at this point.

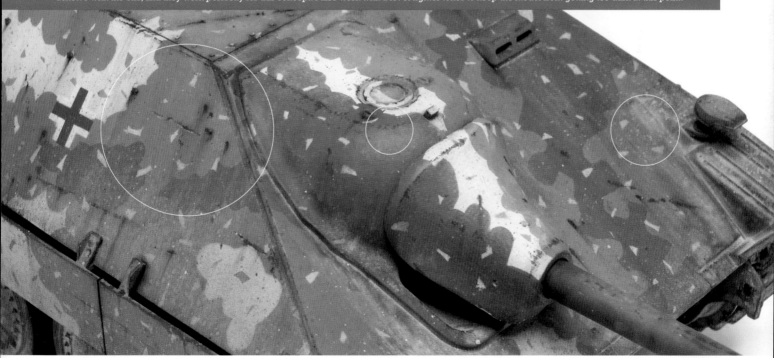

JAGDPANZER 38(t) HETZER

thoughts on layering basic weathering processes to achieve greater depth:

• on a project like this one where it contains less steps to arrive at the final results, there is still trmemndous amount that can be done with these simple steps. Working between multiple layers of dust, dirt and OPR is the best to create depth to the weathering. I rarely stop at one application of any step, and often use two, three even more layers of a process to get to where I want it to look.

• there are also no hard rules, just guidelines. For example, I add dust colored oils into the main panel lines that were already given dark pinwashes, and other times I add stains into the dust pigments to create softer diffused marks. I do this all over the model constantly working to make each section of the model as good as possible.

• and don't be afraid of mistakes, they are usually small at this point, and can be easily incorporated with minor additional effort.

in service systems should be rusty but the metal is still very much intact, thus paint like these are more accurate to represent the state of the exhausts on a combat tank.

This particular variant of the Hetzer as made by Tamiya is what is considered the Middle Production version and the single large exhaust lays uncovered on the rear engine deck, fully exposed. Perfect! Any untreated steel thin-walled tubing will quickly surface rust under high temps and moisture exposure, so this makes the procedure very straight forward --and yes, tons of fun!

○ Thin dust layers is applied with oils and pigments to add contrast to the cleaner darker hatch areas.

○ This area is worn specifically to illustrate the missing antenna wires were originally stored here and left marks in the paint.

○ The rear taillight is painted a glossy blue color to replicate the real light. Also note the thinned exhuast muffler opening.

• it's a common happening that while the weathering is progressing the model itself is speaking to you visually at each step of the way. Sometimes when you review your work as it goes, you will see new avenues to explore. Here the top plate of the hull really became an obvious point of attention to fade the colors on one hand, and to tint the paint to add even more contrast between the tonal values.

• to fade paint, you do not necessarily need to just add lighter colors, by applying a dark tone to border it with, the greater values will give you even more visual contrast pushing the lighter tones brighter, and the middle-to-dark tones darker across a broader range.

• and again, to further reinforce the point, layering the colors is the best method to achieve the level of depth and interest within any given area, as seen in these photos.

While painting the exhuast, I wanted to have some of the camo paint remain, so I focused my rust layers on the upper half of the muffler cyclinder. The process is simple, thin the LC Rust paints with water (I'd say around 60-40), and then brush it on. Layer the colors up, one on top of the other from light to dark, and you can also use a small piece of sponge to create additional layered effects. At the very end, I use the sponge and the Rust Dark Shadow color and dry-sponge some fine dots with non-thinned paint to have a final layer of tiny dark spots. I then go back over the top layers with a touch more of the lighter yellow tone to apply some very fresh rust stains and streaks.

PIGMENTS, ROUND 2

Unlike the TIger model, the second round of pigments was not dictated by a desire to redo the weathering, yet rather out of necessity because once the road wheels and tracks are glued on in their weathered state, I added the side skirts after, and then the rest of the model can be also dirtied up at this time. But now the various painted detials, chips, etc. can be blended in all together under the next round of pigments.

○ The right side of the model is intentionally weathered differently than the other side, because this concept provides a greater level of story telling and makes a simple stand alone model have greater life.

○ **thoughts on balancing the weathering versus the paintjob:**

• creating a cohesive project with the weathering of an already complicated ambush camo scheme is a tricky thing to achieve. It's best to keep the painted colors visible and clear to a large degree, and keep the heavier weathering down low. The point of this project was the paintjob, so the weathering must play to that goal, otherwise it's a waste of time unless you have a very specific reference photo to model from. I prefer to let the harmony of the painting and weathering coexist so I can both enjoy the intricate camo scheme, and still have a properly used combat vehicle that expresses the subject nicely.

○ Looking down on the model the weathering is clearly built up from the bottom to the top of the hull in a steady progression that matches the heavily sloped shape of the Hetzer.

○ Tonal variations are applied throughout the weathering with OPR. The colors are simplified to maintain the balance of the model.

○ Both the tracks and the hull pigments are heavier and more opaque on the left side of the hull, all intentionally presented to tell the story of the vehicle.

thoughts on story telling and deadlines to help us complete a project:

• story telling is an element inherent in what scale modeling is all about. Using the painting and weathering is paramount to having success with that idea and I am constantly thinking about it. Where can I add something? How can I improve the look of this area, or that? It doesn't really stop even though it must at some point. As a professional, this is often a deadline, but for others it may be a competition show, or a club meeting. It must be said some form of deadline is worthwhile to use to create a start and end point for us to work within. This OOB project had a simpler goal in mind that focused around its unique paint scheme. Using similar elements of the process help us to finish models in a reasonable amount of time.

The first order of business is to give the model a dusty look, (I had descided to maintain a late springtime/summer style of dusting to show muddy areas, but not heavy winter style mud buildup). So I start by dusting the hull one section at a time. I use the same process of light dusting that I used on the Tiger where I apply the dust pigments to the model dry using only a little bit on the brush, scrubbing it in a natural fashion, then airbrushing a liquid fixer in a very light misting pattern from farther away letting the fixer mist down upon the pigments and setting them in place. I repeat the process a few more times to build up the dust opacity slowly until I'm happy with the look. I then layer additional stains to create a better sense of depth to the finish.

Now I can break out some oil paints and add the final touches to the weathering. I use the oils to fade and alter certain panel tones to break up the model a bit more, plus I add more subtle streaks and stains to the surface concentrating on making the Jagdpanzer look well used, but not excessively so.

As I am doing this, I feel the model needs that last bit of interest to pull it all together. Hetzers rarely had any external stowage added, so my last weathering efforts are executed with pigments again. This time I went for a very intentional level of asymmetry across the hull from one side to the other. I reasoned that in a very similar fashion to driving a car along a road and half the car drives through a large puddle on one side only, so to I felt I could splash pigments along the left side in a way that clearly illustrates this common occurence when driving around. I imagined this late-war Hetzer hustling along a lone dirt road on its way to position itself for a final defense of its home town. I loaded an old brush with wet pigments and proceeded to make it happen.

○ The final element of weathering with the pigments creates the most lasting impression upon the model.

thoughts on the final elements that bring it all together:

• from my industrial design education and learning how to create realistic renderings of vehicles, it was often the last stages of a drawing that while small in relation to the rest of the efforts, this final 5% often provided a disproportionate amount of success towards the end result. Here on this model, the left side skirt and its mud splatters were such a defining element to the visual effects, yet were achieved with a simple form of flicking a brush loaded with wet pigments. I repeated the process and adjusted the angle of the flicking action to create the muddied areas, simple as it was, but the results transformed the model to a much more interesting project that immediately drew in the viewer. Ideas like this are one of the most rewarding aspects to the process, and often come only moments prior to the action. It wasn't premeditated beyond I knew the model needed some element that stood out from the rest. Once a viewer had absorbed the cool ambush camo scheme, the model still needed another level of interest to speak back to the viewer. The simple mud splatters work to tell a story of the subject, and this is a fundamental step in any model building project, stand alone vehicles or dioramas, it must be present to have success.

○

Gerät 555

This project was defined by three elements; one, utilizing a kit that is exceptional and hassle free, plus very accurate, two, sticking to an OOB build and then focus mainly on the third element, the ambush camo scheme common to the subject. How one element affects the other resulted in a cohesive model that allowed for maximum energy to be spent most efficiently. Not having to worry about the construciton of the kit gave me the mental freedom to think about and execute the complicated camoflage in a very accurate, if not a bit tedious manner. And then the simpler turretless shape of the Hetzer, allowed me to use more traditional weathering methods to enhance the paintjob without overwhelming it. Striking a balance between them all is a very unique perspective and one I feel worthy of such discussion.

I speak to the need to enjoy scale modeling at its most basic elements. To not get overwhelmed with every kit to represent the ultimate endeavor. Taking a step sideways perhaps (not really backwards), and utilizing what is available in quality form and then proceed to enjoy the execution stages much more completely. Less stress is relevant, we often get concerned with fixing this or that part, trying to use every new or latest painting process, and this can be counter productive in the overall scheme of hobby enjoyment. TANKART is not solely about recreating every project to a extremely high level, it is always about artistic scale-ism and that comes in many flavors. Here this wonderful Hetzer kit provided an amazing building experience needing only a minor mod here and there, and then recreating the ambush scheme was also very rewarding to achieve a true to scale paintjob, and finally the weathering where time honored techniques proved just as valuable as always.

JAGDPANZER 38(t) für

Jgd Pz 38(t) Hetzer für 7.5cm PaK39 L/48

7.5cm PaK39 HETZER

PRIMER

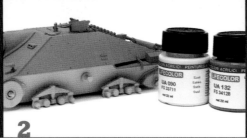

BASE COAT

STENCILS

SPRAY MASK CAMO

DETAIL PAINTING

APPLY MARKINGS

FILTER

BROWN PINWASH

PINWASH AND STREAKS

BLEND STREAKS

DARK PINWASH

ROAD WHEELS PINWASH

TANK

QUICK REF SBS

INITIAL PIGMENTS

METAL CHIPPING

CHIPPING & SCRATCHES

EXHAUST - LAYER 1

EXHAUST - LAYER 2

EXHAUST - LAYER 3

EXHAUST - LAYER 4

FINAL EXHAUST

MORE PIGMENTS

ASSYMETRICAL PIGMENTS

OPR FADING, STREAKS & STAINS

FINAL MUD SPLATTERS

Sd Kfz 251/22 mit 7.5cm PaK40 L/46 Pakwagen

Sd.Kfz 251/22

The dominant scale in the armor modeling community is clearly 1/35, followed closely by 1/72, but the recent emergence of 1/48 as a revived scale for armor kits is a very interesting situation. Tamiya took it upon themselves to bring back this scale as a new series of kits originally intended to bridge the gap for the large population of 1/48 aircraft modelers, both to obtain cross-over sales and to increase the ability to make effective aircraft and armor dioramas together, which is quite popular in Japan.

This makes perfect sense to Tamiya because they are a top producer of 1/48 aircraft kits, and like their armor kits they are industry leaders in the category. To date they have focused almost solely on WWII German armor releases and that was the starting point for this project. I have always desired to build a Sd.Kfz 251/22 Pakwagen, but both the 1/35 Dragon and AFV Club kits required some extra work to create a quality model, both kits are decent, but both have issues as well. So I turned to another solution and that was presented when Gasoline announced a new resin 1/48 conversion of the Pakwagen for the 1/48 Tamiya Sd.Kfz 251/1 Ausf. D kit. Problem solved, and I decided to head down that road instead.

To date, I have built a few of the new 1/48 kits prior to this one, all OOB projects, and I must admit to liking them quite a lot. They are just large enough to enjoy the painting and weathering, and they can still be detailed to rival the larger 1/35 kits without spending as much money, or taking as much time. They are like 1/35-lite kits! But I wanted a bigger challenge, so I set about to see if I could fool the eye. Could I paint and weather a 1/48 kit to be as exact as a larger 1/35 model?

CHÜTZENPANZERWAGEN
[7.5cm PaK40]

TAMIYA QUALITY

Regardless of what model company is being discussed, it is hard to ignore that any conversation about how a kit goes together, its fit and finish, is rarely not compared to what we have come to expect from the steel molds of Tamiya. In today's market we have many new manufacturers and more than a few have risen to equal and sometimes surpass Tamiya, but Tamiya has usually been associated with that benchmark of quality the rest get compared to.

Certainly they are not nearly as aggressive in the armor market as in previous years, but that does not dimish the actual build quality of what kits they do produce. It is not so much a question of who is better, but more to the point of how best to produce a worthy kit for public consumption, and I feel Tamiya have historically been the bar all others are judged by. I can't remember the last time Tamiya had an actual error in the instructions, or a boxart was not worth of hanging on the wall, or the parts on the sprue were not exceptionally molded and once trimmed and sanded for assembly, the construction was precise and effective. This left room for me to decide what details to add or ignore, and more importantly to get to the painting and weathering stages in a hassle-free manner, which is obviously an area I spend a lot of time in.

But that is just opinion of course, when the glue hits the plastic that is when the conversation is a moot point and becoming a modeler is far more important, no matter good or bad the kit is. These 1/48 kits, love or hate them, live up to all of their larger 1/35 cousins and indeed provide a worthy template to work in. The aftermarket companies have also provided excellent upgrades as well, and here I used Gasoline's resin conversion to create this variant. And it all starts with preparing the plastic bits for the additional of the resin parts.

○ Abandoned and ill-treated this Pakwagen's service is only as a road side monument.

• within every model I try to find some element that will either be the focus of my efforts, or create an artificial challenge so I can push myself further and attempt projects that I have not yet tried. This might seem unusual to some, say for instance, I don't focus my modeling on one theater or operation, or stick to one side of the conflict or the other. My modeling interests are probably considered quite general and I like a great many different subjects. It comes at a price because I tend to not be an expert in any one area, save the painting and weathering processes, but I also have the pleasure to expand my horizons and work on a wide selection of models. So in that regards, I find challenges in researching new subjects and also in ways to affect my painting efforts. One trick I use is to step down a scale to test myself. When working in a larger scale, we get used to a certain level of detail and accuracy, but by forcing a smaller scale build into the mix, we tostle this notion and it requires extra attention to acheive a similar level of finish as the larger models. Up until this project, I had used the hairspray technique quite a few times with a lot of success, and within my research I came across a Pakwagen photos that showed a heavily worn vehicle at war's end that had been sitting abandoned for quite some time. Keen to try my hand at recreating the subject, I knew only one process that would truly give the results I was after. I actually knew it the moment I saw the photo, I had to pick up the challenge and started the build without any further hesitation, as I had a very clear end game in mind when this model began.

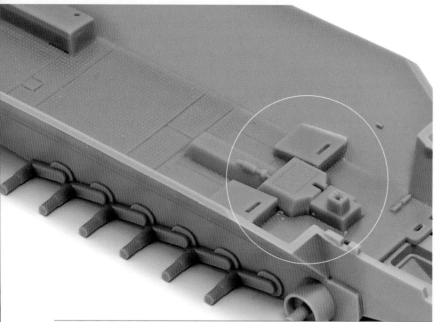

Construction starts immediately with the first pieces of resin are fitted into the of the hull.

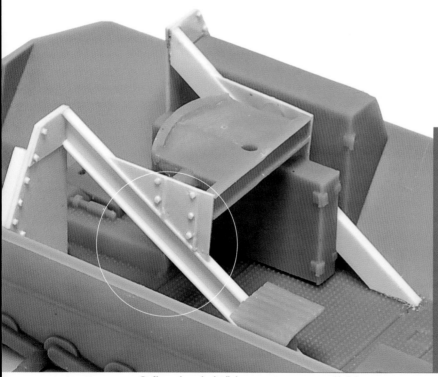

New and superior detailed gun support mounts are scratchbuilt from styrene.

CHASSIS CONSTRUCTION

Almost immediately with the project, adding the resin parts was a necessity. I focused on the hull build up and left the simple suspension areas for later both for easier handling and to clear any fitment issues present in resin parts right away, focusing my energy into the clean-up of these parts and to dry the major resin pieces and make adjustments to ensure they fit as well I can make them. The Gasoline parts are largely blemish free and cast straight and true, so that is great to not spend much time straightening the parts and fixing casting errors. The first bits fit into the lower hull area without too much hassle, but once I got to the gun mount itself I was less impressed.

Like any good project, it all starts with proper reference and I had the older, yet still excellent, Sturm & Drang Japanese language book on the Sd.Kfz 251 series and inside there was both the image I wanted to paint the model like, and it also had some good images of how the gun looked sitting in the chassis. I wasn't keen on the Gasoline solution, so I took the scratchbuilding route instead and made styrene support mounts to integrate with the resin parts in a more accurate fashion. The resin parts were also too simplified for my tastes, even though the idea behind 1/48 kits is to utilize a simpler detail level to speed up the construction process. Here because I was adding extra effort into the conversion I felt it prudent to make the added parts in a more presentable fashion, especially since this model is an open top vehicle and these specific areas will definitely be seen afterwards.

thoughts on 1/48 armor compared to 1/35 kits:

• a new element to our daily model kit diet are these cool 1/48 Tamiya kits, but how do they really stack up. For those of used to the larger 1/35 kits, I found the details close to the larger kits, with little lost in the end due to some simplification. Fit and finish are as the 1/35 kits, but Tamiya makes efforts to improve the tracks in particular. I've never been a fan of 1-piece rubber/vinyl tracks and here we get very nice injected plastic link-and-length tracks that make the process so much nicer and easier to deal with. Other than filling some ejector pin marks on them, which due to their size is not a major issue, the fit and final look are excellent. Subjects with track sag have it molded into the parts, so in the end we get a wonderful model that looks as good as some of the 1/35 kits. Plus, a host of aftermarket is readily available from resin and PE companies, including Friul tracks for a few subjects. So 1/48 is a nice scale to definitely give a try, the available kits are worth another look.

thoughts on improving the gun mount:

• I was not happy with the gun supports in the Gasoline resin conversion and there were some fitment and detail issues with the angled bulkhead too, so my efforts were turned to recreating better parts in styrene. I used the resin parts as a guide, and photos as reference to scratch superior details and arrive at a more accurate representation of this area. The open top nature dictated this change and the effort goes quick enough due to the smaller size of the parts in question. Styrene I-beams and 90 deg corner lengths were put to good use to achieve the look I saw in the photos. The resin parts were formed from flat square sections and are inaccurate to the real vehicle.

○ The finished gun assembly with metal barrel. It's simple, yet captures the look of the 7.5cm gun well.

○ The gun test fitted into the new mount, it's height relative to the hull was a key element to get right.

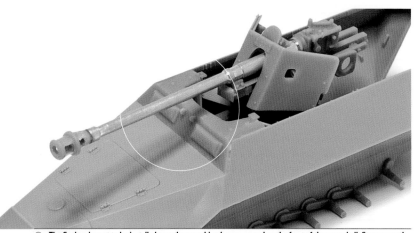

○ The final resin part to be installed was the new driver's armor panel on the front of the upper hull, fit was great!

○ The track and road wheels assembled as one unit for each side to facilitate the painting process.

So with what limited reference I had, I create the improved support arms and gun mounts, added them to the resin parts and fit the assembly inside the hull. Fortunately, the gun itself was an excellent collection of resin and metal parts and I no issues with it, building it up as a stand alone subassembly for easier painting. Yes, it was simplified, but did capture the look enough for me.

After I had finished the new gun mount, I test fitted everything including the upper hull to lower fitment to ensure I had done it correctly, which thankfully was the case. I also glued in the new front upper hull armor panel, which fit near perfectly with little effort. It's unique shape is design to allow limited side-to-side gun traverse. The gun sat in the mount on its own, and was removable for painting.

Now I turned my attention to the front suspension, tracks and road wheels. The front suspension is simplistic by nature and goes together very easily and quite fast, as well as the excellent front wheels, which are left loose for painting. Next, I prepped all the road wheels and the link-and-length tracks for assembly. There is no right or wrong way to build up this area, so if you feel more comfortable adding the tracks after the fact, or using a combination of both ideas and leave off the outer road wheels for example, it all works OK in the end. It's more of a personal preference and how you use your processes. If you've never tried it this way before, give it a shot to see if you like it. This area is small regardless, so it doesn't take long to get it all together and the top track runs have some gentle sag worked into them, which are then glued down to the top of the raod wheels to hold it in place. Each side is then slipped onto the axles to dry and for my photo sessions.

○ **tips for working with open top models for easier painting:**

• open top models are similar to aircraft modeling in that we need to finalize the interior painting and weathering before we can close the hull and paint the exterior. Always a bit of pain honestly, there are some processes that makes this job a bit easier to manage.

• work in sub-assemblies and break the model down into the fewest number possible. Here I had the lower hull will all the fittings below the centerline in place, and then the upper hull, and finally the gun itself.

• Even though you can see most details, if you are careful you can focus your efforts on areas easier to see if time and energy expended are considerations. Each of us models differently and the possiblities are limited only by what you attempt to achieve. I knew this model was to be presented in an abandoned state and that is how I proceeded to work the painted details. It also eliminated the need to outfit the inside with all of the crew gear, combat details, and ammunition. How the 7.5cm shells were actually stored in the Pakwagen is a bit of a mystery, so it was nice to not worry about that element.

• while the photo above is presented full page the model is less than half this actual size and thus that driver's compartment is tiny and will all but disappear once the upper hull is fitted, and the large gun is in place. Tamiya get this and provide us with the basics to fill the space. And as we know well, each of has different ideas on how best to work that idea, do we go all out and really super-detail the area, as much for the modeling satisfaction versus the need to see it, or do we work with what is there and let the paint be good enough? I choose the later more often than not, but that's not a negative, just a different point of view on how best to finalize a project like this. I would likely put more effort into a larger 1/35 half-track project, but here the size and severely limited viewpoint makes it an easy decision for me.

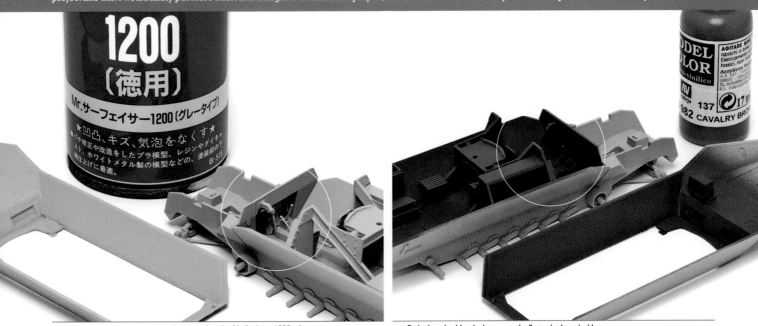

○ Interior paint prep was performed with my favorite Mr. Surfacer 1200 primer.

○ Red primer is airbrushed to create the first paint layer inside.

139

INTERIOR PAINTING

It all begins inside, as they say. Planning the paintjob on the model, like I said previously, I knew the process that I was going to use in my mind from the word go. It had to be done with the HS technique because I was certainly not going to apply marks of any kind that come even close to being in-scale in 1/48. I had used HS enough times prior to this model to understand it's true power and I was fully excited to put into action. I was confident it was up to the task at hand, so with that in mind, I primed the interior areas with Mr. Surfacer 1200 and then laid down a layer of red primer paint with Vallejo's Model Color Cavalry Brown, which I use straight the bottle thinned about 50-50 with water. This would be the color of the interior chips and scratches, and on top of this I sprayed my HS in my usual manner of two even layers.

After the HS was dry, I could then apply the Dunkelgelb interior color. I used Tamiya XF-60 Dark Yellow with a few drops of XF-55 Deck Tan added to tone the color down a bit, which was airbrushed on to cover the interior in a solid opaque layer. I then add a bit more Deck Tan to this mix, thin it a little more, and then do some minor highlighting and fading, just enough to break up the single color a little more. And due to the diminuitive size of the model, this all proceeds at a rapid pace, such is the way with modeling in 1/48. Did I mention that it is also a lot faster modeling episode at this scale?

○ Interior painting via the HS technique with the leather bench covers hand painted afterwards.

○ **tips on painting and weathering open top combat vehicles:**

• interior painting is never quite the same as exterior efforts, but working with an open top half-track fighting compartments definitely helps so we can enjoy some heavier weathering processes. A lot of these very finely molded details are not even seen until some serious wear and tear is given to them, and suddenly the interior volumes really jump out at you.

• I start with the chipping and scratches and try to keep them human sized because most marks will be generated by the crew itself and not outside elements. For example, I added scratches where the loading and removal of the ammo shells from the storage bin might impact the hull sides, being large heavy metal objects. The floor is also an obvious candidate and here I add the most weathering in the form of pigments, washes and thicker oil paint stains. Something simple like water dripping from a canteen while the crewman drinks can turn dirt on the floor to a dirty mess, so I try to think along those lines when I am applying the stains.

• I tend to downplay the other weathering effects for the interior in an effort to keep them more in-scale, because overworked interiors can be counter-productive to a successful model, the balance of realism is just as pivotal inside as it is outside.

○ Once weathered up with pigments and oils, the interior really comes to life.

• weathering inside the fighting compartment was actually quite enjoyable, the color tones of this project allow for good contrast to be built up. This process is the same as how I consider the exterior when I am working with the philosophy of layering effects on top of each other to arrive at a final result. It is simply done with more conservative efforts to mitigate any chances of over doing these areas. I look at it as more of an additional visual databank for the viewer when they peer over the edges to look inside the hull. The exterior draws them and the unique finish keeps them interested, and then the final layer is the exposed interior, so I tend to want their reactions to be in a progression, rather than a jolt once they see the finished interior.

With the Dunkelgelb applied, I could begin to add the chips and scratches on the inside surfaces. Naturally the process is actually one of removal, but the concept is the same. I start at the edges and wet a small section with water, then slowly work my way around the model in this fashion to create the paint wear. The floor received a bit more more effort, and overall I was happy how it turned out. One thought with chipping a solid opaque paint layer is that you have fewer chips appear, which is preferrable, and they will be sharp and visually strong (why it's best there are fewer of them). Other marks are created with sharper tools like a toothpick, which has sharp edges but is still smooth enough to not damage the surrounding paint.

The upper hull glued in place after the interior is completed, and again the fit was perfect.

141

paint callouts for the Pakwagen project:

• RED PRIMER: As described in the previous chapters, I like how *Vallejo Model Color Cavalry Brown 982* looks out of the bottle.

• GREY PRIMER: A great choice is *Tamiya XF-24 Dark Grey* mixed with a few drops *XF-69 NATO Gray*, plus a drop of *XF-7 Flat Red*.

• DUNKELGELB: On this Pakwagen project I used *Tamiya XF-60 Dark Yellow* with a few drop of *XF-55 Deck Tan* to cut the greenish tint down a little for the interior painting. For the exterior, I swapped in *XF-3 Flat Yellow* for the Deck Tan, and then added some *XF-2 Flat White* for the lightening element.

• PALE CAMO GREEN: I use a mixture of *Tamiya XF-5 Flat Green* and the exterior Dunkelgelb recipe above to create a pale green color. I prefer adding basecoat colors to the camo colors as a good way to lighten them up a bit.

quick ref:

- **RED PRIMER:**
  Cavalry Brown 982

- **GREY PRIMER:**
  XF-24 Dark Grey
  XF-69 NATO Gray
  XF-7 Flat Red

- **DUNKELGELB:**
  XF-60 Dark Yellow
  XF-55 Deck Tan
  XF-3 Flat Yellow
  XF-2 Flat White

- **CAMO GREEN:**
  XF-5 Flat Green
  mixed with the
  Dunkelgelb

EXTERIOR PAINTING

The exterior process mimiced the interior paint procedure in more or less the same fashion. For this stage I had my one main reference photo at hand constantly checking to get as close to the heavy wear and tear as I could muster. It was the primary focus of this project so achieving that level of quality and scale in my efforts was of paramount importance, it truly was a challenge due to the limited surface area present in this smaller model.

I know that I will be using Tamiys paints as well. Once thinned with water and applied over the HS layers, it will give me the best chance of success with the chips and scratches due to the manner in which it comes off. This was probably the single most critical HS paint chipping that I had done to date, and while I knew in my head it would work as intended, the pressure was certainly on to perform.

With those thoughts in my head, I proceeded to prime models exterior subassemblies. I first taped off the inner edge of the exposed interior and then filled the main hole in with tissue to protect it from any overspray that could easily ruin my interior painting efforts. I follow the

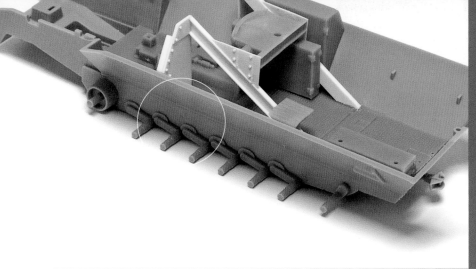

tips for using red and gray primer colors :

• I choose to paint the red primer as actual. I do this for the reason that I produce the red chips via the hairspray method, so it makes sense to start with it as the first color layer.

• I tend to lean towards a more true red and slightly brighter color because when the chips are very small they remain visible and look like red primer. Too dark of a color choice and the chips will look more like rusted metal than red primer.

• It is well known that German main gun barrels were primed in a heat resistant dark gray primer. I choose to have this color a "warmer" tone than Panzergrau (which I tint slightly cooler with blues). Thus I add a drop of red to the grey to give it this tint.

○ All the exterior subassemblies are given proper primer coverage with Mr. Surfacer 1200.

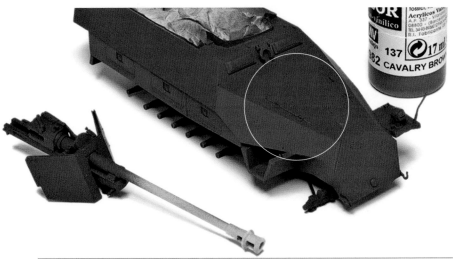

○ The primer is followed by a red primer undercoat using Vallejo's excellent Cavalry Brown color.

○ Two even hairspray layers go on next -- the model is now set to receive its camoflage.

primer just as I did before with the Cavalry Brown for my red primer choice. I then mask off the back of the gun and spray the barrel itself in a dark gray paint to represent the heat resistent barrel primer commonly used and seen in reference photos.

HS TECHNIQUE

It's now time to get serious and buckle down, I am ready to begin the main phase of the entire operation. It starts with my now routine process of spray two layers of HS, drying each and then the model is prepped for the basecoat of Dunkelgelb.

For this color, I wanted a slightly different tonal value to the color I used on the inside, so this time I add a bit of Tamiya XF-3 Flat Yellow to the XF-60 Dark Yellow as my base Dunkelgelb. I spray it opaque enough to cover properly, but anywhere as referenced in my photo that showed heavy chipping I back off on the coverage to leave a hint of the red primer showing through, similar to how whitewash is sprayed so the resulting chips will be much finer and gradiate out from those areas. These were mostly concentrated around the rear of the hull. This step was key, and I cannot emphasis this detail enough, otherwise the chips would have been too large and too strong not giving me the worn look I saw in the photo. This was also true of the barrel, I barely covered it in fact, because I knew most of it was coming off in the chipping stage.

With the first painting pass completed, I then added some XF-2 Flat White to my paint mix, plus a few drops of water to thin it even more and then sprayed some faded areas and streaks across the upper hull

○ The Dunkelgelb is mixed from the above Tamiya paints and thin with water for superior chipping results.

thoughts on spraying basecoat designed to be chipped using the HS technique:

• I spent a considerable amount of time and energy in the early days of using hairspray for chipping to figure out its strengths and weaknesses. For example, thinning Tamiya acrylics with lacquer thinner provides an excellent method to spray these paints, however, its adhesion qualities also skyrocket making this process unsuitable for use with HS layers underneath. The water simply can't get below such a top layer of paint, so I decided to thin the Tamiya paints with water instead, which reduces the adhesion level to a more reasonable amount, and this provides a much better method to chip away with.

○ The model after the basecoat is lightened and the green camo added, ready to be chipped.

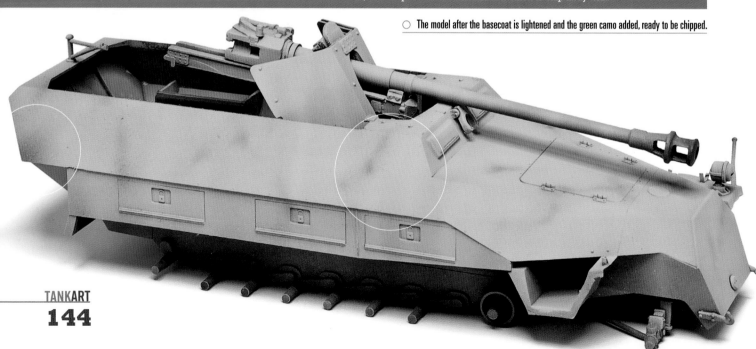

and down the sloped sides. With the base coat complete, I clean my airbrush and then load a heavily thinned pale green camo color and spray very very faint green camoflage spots to the model.

And now the real fun begins. Not wasting any time, I begin the all important chipping process. With my reference nearby, I start at the right rear corner and gradually work my way down the sides of the hull in an effort to capture as much of the chipping and scratches as possible. Relief does start to set in as the procedure goes off without a hitch and the paint wear is coming out exactly as I intended, and most importantly the marks are in-scale. I make good use of my brushes, but it was the Tamiya Paint Stir Stick (seen above) that really came into its own. I used it to start chips and also to apply those long linear horizontal scratches. To do this, I used a small piece of wood a couple of inches thick to rest my hand on as I moved the stick across the surface of the model, acting as a bridge to steady my hand's movement.

tips for achieving chipping and scratching success and the tools used to do it with:

• the photo above illustrates the tools I use to chip my models. I have used the two brushes from the very first HS technique model until this day. The flat brush is used to apply the water and I use it for finer chipping, and the short bristled brush is one I actually cut the bristles down with to make a short scruffy brush and is the main brush I use in the majority of my chipping projects. I use other brushes too, but these are my two primary ones.

• a relatively new addition to my HS chipping tool stable is the *Tamiya Paint Stir Stick*, which is actually chromed plated metal. And this is what makes it so perfect for the task. I use it more than toothpicks now for scratches. The two ends are different shaped, and while sharp to the touch, the chrome plating makes it very smooth and this reduces its ability to damage the model further. By using a delicate touch, the edge of round spoon creates perfect scratches in the top layer of paint, and is what I used to make the long scratches seen above.

• any time you require linear effects, I find it helps enormously use what is called a bridge to help steady your hand as it moves sideways. This method improves accuracy as well to help you place the tool right where you want it to move across.

• I work quite slowly when I am doing the chipping process. The small model size definitely helped speed it along, but usually it takes a few days or evenings to properly cover a model the right way. I don't like to rush my motions and I move the brushes and tools in a controlled fashion, and this goes a long ways to preventing large flaked chips when you least expect or desire them on the model. Rarely is this the look you are going for.

tips for finishing off the chipped areas to complete the look:

• once the model is chipped (regardless of the actual method used to create them), there is still quite a bit to do to truly make them look realistic. Micro-chipping, as it is now called, is the main process to add to any layered chipped procedure. It requires some good quality fine-tipped brushes, and some good eyewear if your eyes are fading like mine. I always do this step with the trusty Optivisor in place. Remember this model is only 1/48 and while the photos are reproduced in large format, the model itself is only a few inches long, as attested to by the giant oversized Lifecolor bottle shown below for scale effect.

• the layered chip principle is very simple. You begin with the lightest color, and work your way to the center with darker colors to ultimately represent bare metal, if that is your goal. It was here due to the abandoned nature of the project, so I use a dark brown color with a hint of gray to it, and as you can see I have a handy pre-mixed paint normally used for painting tracks. The colors are perfect for this model, and using the #2 round brush, I very carefully paint inside the largest of the red primer chips to illustrate how the paint is worn through to the metal surface. The color thus represents the dark rust tones steel armor take on when exposed for long periods of time. I am intentionally reinforcing the notion that this is a derelict vehicle, and the reference photos support this end result -- an ever important element to the success of this process.

With the right side of the hull completed and my confidence working hard, I continue around the entire model in one sitting, thankful for the smaller size of this kit. I felt since I was really in the groove and the chips were coming out as I wanted them to, I had to keep going. It did take a few hours, but it was really worth it, and I chipped the main gun and the road wheels as well.

Afterwards, I breathed a lot easier and then added the side markings, a simple unit number sprayed through some Eduard German vinyl masks, and I used the trick to spot spray some HS in those two areas so I could chip the numbers as well, which worked perfectly. I also added some very faint residual whitewash areas, making this an early 1945 springtime vehicle. Again, I used a touch of HS under those areas, sprayed a tiny amount of white paint over them, and then wore it off as before, all intended to give the model just a hint more visual interest and you almost don't see them at first.

○

thoughts on weathering abandoned armor models:

• painting is the essential process by which we really illustrate the situation the model is intended to represent. I had a clear vision to display this model as an abandoned vehicle and the way in which the paint is shown is a key element to the viewer understanding my concept.

• the colors are less saturated, it has been standing still for days, even longer perhaps, and the faded nature is more encompassing overall. There is also far less dirt being thron onto to the paint because of the lack of movement through the field, so pimwashes should take this into account and finally weather washes most of this away and the water simply continues to fade the paint, as does the sun.

○ Pinwashes are applied to shadow in what limited details are present on the surface.

○ Pale filters were used to deaden the colors and create a more muted visual effect.

tips for achieving quality filter layers: ○

• filters play a small, but key, role in the weathering process, and are used to good effect in cases like this project where I wanted a relatively muted look but did not want to resort to fading the paint in the airbrushing stages. Trying to do that is far more difficult to succeed with, and using filters provides us with a much greater chance of achieving the desired results.

• fortunately, fading Dunkelgelb is a rather easy task because it doesn't require much effort to do so. Yellows tint very easily, plus they respond a variety of filter colors to go any direction you choose. It can be rich and deeper via darker oranges and browns; or like here, can be muted out with pale gray tones and light ochre colors. Always practice on scrap if you are unsure what you want, and once applied dry them completely before proceeding to the next step.

SD KFZ 251/22 PAKWAGEN

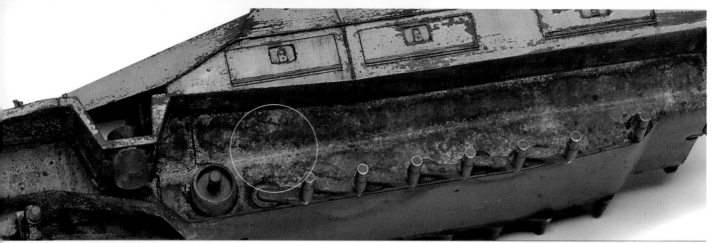

○ Use of pigments was limited to the lower hull areas only, and I only wanted enough coverage to give the model the impression it hadn't been used in a long time.

○ I made the best of the opportunity that I had a missing right front fender and gave this area extra attention. I used some thinner to add these additional streaks in the pigments.

thoughts on the later phases of assembly, and how it relates to the finishing steps being used: ○

• projects of this nature that require painting and further assembly as it moves along are more of a challenge in both keeping everything in order and balanced overall, but also with motivation and seeing it completed faithfully. Open top vehicles are a bit like doing two models at once, and this can have negative affects on finishing them in a timeframe that provides satisfaction. Painting goals help a lot with this because it helps us to stay organized throughout the process, and it also moves it along to the next steps. Same with the weathering. For example, doing the pinwash stage meant I really needed to see the track and road wheel assemblies mounted on the model so I can add the washes to that section too and get a better feel for my progress. To get there meant I had to have them painted and ready to be weathered, and this kept me moving forward. Try to use the processes themselves to keep the drive going in the project. It's not always possible, but tricks like this can definitely help us get there.

○ The model at the early weathering stages. All of the paint wear and tear has been completed, and the filter and pinwashes successfully applied.

thoughts on using OPR to successfully finalize the paintjob: ○

• this project, in particular, was an excellent candidate to fully utilize OPR and I put a lot of effort into reworking the paint to gain the maximum results from the process. So much hinged on how well I portrayed the model in an abandoned state, and the oils were perfect to really give the finish that sort of look.

• I made my palette with as many colors as I felt would give me maximum choices, even if I used some of them only once or twice on the model, it was better to have them handy than not. Naturally, a few of these colors got more usage, but in general, I try to use a specific color for certain effects. Various brown tones mixed with grays were important for the dirtier areas and this blended well with the gray filters I used previously. And because I am using almost no thinner at all, there is no worry about reactivating the enamel filter, once it was dry it is OK to proceed with the oil applications.

• I always work with OPR in sections using all the colors I want in that area at a time. In other words, I do not apply one oil at a time to all of the parts of the model I think it will go. Rather, I complete an entire section first with as much as I deem necessary, and then I move onto the next area. The results are more complete and easier to maintain control over. Because of this I typically have 4-5 brushes in my hands and one in my mouth as I work, simply grabbing what color brush I want and using it, then doing my blending after.

With the main part of the model painted, chipped and marked I then could move to the next main phase of the weathering. But before I get to that I do need to get the running gear finsihed and ready to be mounted as well.

The front road wheels are sprayed with in very dark gray color, and then I used a circle template to airbrush both sides in red primer. I follow this with some HS on the outer face of the wheels and then spray my light Dunkelgelb color on top, which was then appropriately chipped like the rest of the model.

For the tracks and main raod assemblies, I had to work these differently to ensure the painting order would come out correctly. I begin by spraying the centers of the road wheels red primer, HS next, then Dunkelgelb, which were these chipped. For the tracks themselves, I simply brushed painted them a pale rust tone with the rubber pads painted a dark gray. I also hand painted the rubber tires on the wheels at the same time, and because these assemblies are quite small it does go rather fast even if it sounds like a fair amount of work. I also take time to paint the odd shaped exhaust muffler on the left front fender too.

○ Fading with the oils is balancing act between adding darker tones against lighter ones.

○ Using what details are present to enhance them in a believable manner is key to success with oils.

○ The final details are painted and weathered to match the rest of the model.

○ Using oil paints, the rusted areas within each chipped area are worked to represent their final look, while the side stowage bins receive darker grime tones to illustrate their constant use.

○ **thoughts on working with oil paints to render the paint details:**

• applying the oil paint to the model is a fundemental process I use that takes the model from the painting stages to its finished form, and the filter and pinwashes simply prepare the surface for the much more involved OPR phase. When I work on a section, I am studying the details and deciding on the colors I want to use by the degree of damage that is present if it's a small chip or scratch, or how dirty I want make that spot and so on. Some parts are also faded, others rusted further.

thoughts on using OPR to take advantage of the surface details and paint wear and tear:

• continuing with this line of thought, specifically I add a tiny dot of color where I want it the strongest, then the I use what blending brush works best for the effect I to create to make that detail the best I can. For example on the small dirt and rust streaks, each oil is placed at the top of the spot, the blending brush is my fine tipped one and then I pull the oil downward leaving the bulk of it at the top of the effect. I do this process each time, determine the color, apply it then blend it out.

○ OPR is put to full affect to rework the paintjob and bring out of the details that have been created so far.

The final model in its ultimate derelict state. Note the different yet subtle tones between the road wheels and the hull, a result of the OPR process.

thoughts on final composition elements that bring the model together in the end:

• the last few efforts are usually what really make the model appear as you had hoped. A model can be 90% completed but still not fully exhibit the look you are going after, and those last details are what bring it all together. Here the rusty green brucke hanging off the rear, the rust details on the gun breech showing it has been unused for some time, the white counting numbers and the caution paint are all part of the group of touches that went into end of the finishing.

• this final weathering effort is complimented by adding some more details to the interior, such as the empty shell casings, spare road wheels and tools left behind, all still to be discovered by the locals or capturing forces soon to move into the region.

○ Additional elements painted earlier are now loaded into the interior, designed to enhance the model's abandoned state.

○ The results of OPR are sometimes very clear such as the streaks, but also are used to enhance the faded whitewash as well.

WEATHERING BEGINS

It was great to finally arrive at this stage with the model looking as it does. I was very satisfied with the efforts I put into the HS chipping and, but I still had the challenge to finish it off to represent an abandoned vehicle, a tricky process in itself.

I start with a filter layer, and here I wanted to deaden the colors a bit, not enhance them or brighten them in any way. I wanted the model to have a flat lifeless look to the paint and used a gray tint and a hint of orange colored filter. I airbrush one nice even layer on the model, dry it off, and move onto the pinwashes next. The exterior is actualy quite simple and void of a lot of details, and combine this with the small size of the model this step too goes fast.

From here I can now break out the oil paints and I use every 502 Abt. color I have that has any relation to the paintjob, 14 in all! In true OPR fashion I basically set about to subtly repaint the entire model. I know that sounds strange, but I go over literally the entire model to fade the paint, dirty it up, tint certain panels, essentially get it to the final finish stages. I also highlight some of the chipped paint edges and add a host of subtle stains and steaks into the paint. Oils were perfect for this and the model was really looking the part now.

But I am not finished just yet, I work up some essential interior bits to strewn about like old tools, empty ammo casings, and a couple of extra road wheels. On the rear of the hull I make a small bucket that is hung from the tow shackle. With this last effort, I decide one element more is needed. When vehicles were left abandoned by roadsides they were given a cautionary markings in bright white so the oncoming traffic would see them at night. I wanted to illustrate an Eastern Frony unit as well, so I spot spray some HS and set about to hand paint the white caution markings, and the white accounting number the Russians painted on derelict vehicles as they advanced West into Germany.

thoughts on the balance of paint colors, the weathering and the added details to arrive at the end result:

• one of the more mental aspects to modeling is the challenge to create a balance between the paintjob, the weathering, and those details either part of both stages or physically added to the model such as stowage. The possibilities are rather endless so narrowing down the elements at work is a crucial decision that directly affects the outcome. I had on this the heavy chipped areas, the soft faint green and white camo spots, the rust spare tracks on the nose, the gun itself and its heavily chipped barrel, the rusting breech, and the small items added to the already weathered interior, on top of which I added the bucket and white caution markings. All of these items and special effects must work together in a compositional aspect and as a balancing act to create a visually interesting model. The story telling process is such a strong parameter to help us achieve this finished level, how it got here, what was taken when the crew left or retreated leaving it as such, whatever the story may have been it is the guiding structure for us to make these very important decisions.

○ The simple act of adding the random items inside the fighting compartment really add to the story telling aspect.

○ The overhead views really capture the many elements that came together in the end, from the interior items strewn about to the white caution markings on the nose.

Sd.Kfz 251/22

I set out to embark upon this project with the goal to really offer my best efforts to see if I was capable of realizing a highly detailed and painted 1/48 model that could rival the finishes normally associated with 1/35 modeling. Could I create a worthy sunject that would be the proper 1/48 canvas to illustrate certain techniques and finishes, and maintain my mantra of artistic scale-ism? This was the challenge that I presented myself in the effort to really push my skill sets to greater levels.

Dropping scales is a fantastic way to hone our craft and while it may not be the scale we work mainly within, these 1/48 kits have a lot of merit on their own, least of all hours of real modeling enjoyment. Which is afterall, part of the reason for doing this hobby. I know it is a large part of why I model. Taking the kit, adding the resin conversion, using my reference to choose the scheme and then executing it are all part of the hobby and what satisfactions I gain from them. For me, I often look at projects like this to develop new ideas and to push old ones more. Our toolbox of techniques is ever evolving and this all plays a hand in how I work and produce the models that I do.

In the end, this model went on to do something very special as well, it achieved a Gold Medal at EuroMilitaire in the single vehicle class and this was a first for a 1/48 model. This achievement is a source of pride and vindication that my goals and challenges of the project were recognized at the highest level of competition. Recognition which fuels my desires to then turn around and share these stories and processes of my many projects with you, so that you too can lay forth a path of similar outline to find the next step of journey in your own scale modeling endeavors.

SD.KFZ 251/22 mittlere

Sd.Kfz 251/22 mit 7.5cm PaK40 L/46 Pakwagen

[7.5cm PaK40]

CHÜTZENPANZERWAGEN

1 PRIMER

2 RED PRIMER

3 HAIR SPRAY

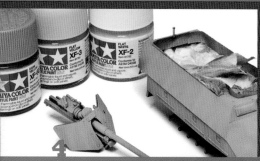

4 BASE COAT

5 CAMO

6 CHIPPING WITH WATER

7 PAINTING STEEL CHIPS

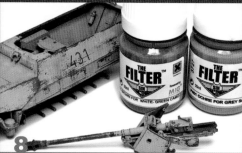

8 FILTERS

9 PIN WASHES

10 PIGMENTS

11 TRACK PAINTING

12 WHEEL PAINTING

QUICK REF SBS

13 CHIPPING DETAILS

14 CHIPPING DETAILS

15 OIL PAINT RENDERING

16 FADED WHITEWASH

17 ENHANCE WASHES

18 STREAKS AND STAINS

19 EXHAUST DETAILS

20 TRACK DETAILS

21 MORE STREAKS AND STAINS

22 FINAL RUST STAINS

23 ADD WHITE HAZARD PAINT

24 PAINT STOWAGE DETAILS

161

Sd.Kfz 161

Any book on modeling German armor would not be complete without showcasing a Panzer IV. The true workhorse of the Panzer divisions, variants of one type or another served from the first day of the war until the last. Over the years we have had some good kits to work with, and like the Tiger I kit from Dragon, their 1/35 Panzer IV series has proven to be a substantial leap in every area that they are the tstandard of the hobby now. The superior technical assistance provided by Tom Cockle and Gary Edmundson have proven key elements in this series, and the resulting products are remarkable scale models.

I was fortunate that my intent to build a Panzer IV coincided with the release of the Dragon early short-barreled Panzer IV Ausf D/E 3-in-1 kit. My interest had been spurred on by the Concord Publications book on the Deusche Afrika Korps (DAK), so this kit was the perfect candidate for what amounts to one of the most intense paintjobs that I have yet attempted -- the impromptu sand over Panzergrau scheme initiated by General Rommel after his first landing in North Africa. Photos of these units are seen within the Concord book and I knew I had to take up the challenge. Anytime field units apply camoflage in such scenarios I am keenly interested because the wear and tear that results from what is essentially a temporary overcoat creates the most wonderful weathering opportunities for us.

The path ahead lies in how the outer paint layer is worn off -- how weather, combat, maintenance and use as a mobile living quarters all interact to arrive at such a finish. I capture it as a moment in time and through the finish I am forever trying to tell the viewer its story. And to successfully do this I have to combine new techniques to achieve the finish that I had in mind, and as seen in the reference photos.

GEN IV AUSF E DAK

○ The imposing well used hulk of the best battle of the German forces in North Africa.

• so much of this project was focused on the theater and the finish associated with it. Desert models take on a life of their own because they do not adhere to more normal painting and weathering routines. What gets used and worn out in the harsh dry climate has a much more unique finish as a result of these very specific circumstances. Using dark rich tones for the washes and pigments doesn't work, you must embrace the starkness, restrict your weathering to maintain the relation to the climate. And while it does mean less work in certain steps as a result, the trick is to balance what effects you do apply to the desert finish without crossing over by doing too much. In fact, I spent most of my time and energy within the painting stages through to the chipping and paint wear, my weathering was quite limited overall.

HISTORY SAYS SO

A few times within the war there are moments regarding paint schemes whereby a crossover of elements creates a unique situation that provides us the modeler with some fantastic opportunities to express a finished model in a truly original paint job. The early DAK units were just such a case and thankfully there is some excellent reference for the purpose of re-creating the look of these units. The story of the Afrika Korps is quite legendary. Combine harsh desert climate and terrain, a toe-to-toe fight with the Allies led by such notaries as General Montegomery and later General Patton, and the interest to work on a piece from this period of action is overwhelming. I personally feel every true WWII armor modeler should have at least one North African desert combatant in their collection, since modeling a desert tank is a cornerstone to having a complete experience in the hobby. The very definition of riding a tank into battle is such a classically romatnic notation during this period of the war, I know I am personally fascinated on multiple levels when studying the two sides.

This first book in the **TANK**ART series starts off with a very late-war Panther clothed in worn whitewash expressing the cold harsh drama of the last desperate days of fighting, and by contrast this Panzer IV in DAK livery illustrates the bookend of ideas with a dry, hot weather and combat beaten tank fighting at the height of the strength of the German armies.

THE BUILD-UP

This model in particular was unique in that I had a very clear idea in my head of its ultimate look long before I started to glue the parts together. I had a road map in mind about the construction process, the modifications and upgrades I wanted to make, and what sort of paintjob I was going to apply to it. It doesn't happen all of the

165

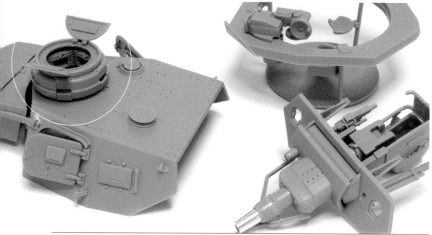

○ The turret assembly is well detailed and the gun superb, all left this way for painting.

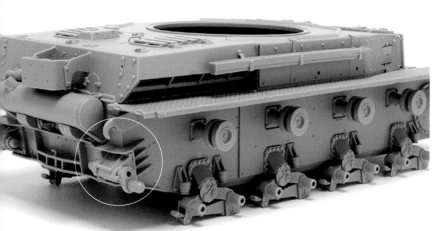

○ Detail of the hull and suspension assemblies are excellent, setting new standards for the Panzer IV series.

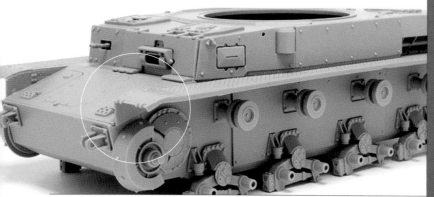

○ This is definitely a model that gets away without using PE fenders, the plastic is well detailed and thin.

time, but I was certainly well prepared for this journey. And I was excited to say the least!

This kit followed closely on the heels of the Tiger I Initial release, so I had a good indication it would be a superb model to work with and it didn't let me down. Yes, it did have some issues, mostly with less than perfect fit in a few spots, but no real negatives and the build is like most in this book of being largely out-of-the-box.

The basic construction was fairly straightforward, but the fact there is a substantial amount of turret interior provided I did have to carefully plan the build and then painting of it. The manner of construction of the front of the turret armor plate that holds the main gun being the tricky part because for an accurate Panzer IV that joint seam of the two parts has a visible weld bead in real life, so I had to work out that process. More on that later.

The rest of the model was built as most tank kits are -- suspension first, then lower hull, the rear fittings, then fenders and joining everything to the upper hull, with the turret being a separate series of subassemblies. This is the early 3-in-1 kit release that exhibited minor fitment issues regarding the fenders and rear hull joints, later Panzer IV kit releases corrected this problem, to Dragon's credit. The kit also provides a metal main gun barrel, a small limited PE fret, and excellent link-to-link plastic tracks, all of which I put to good use. My main areas of attention regarding any changes was to thin the front, rear and side of the fenders and add battle damage, add the fuel can rack, small retaining springs on the rear fenders, and use the PE provided for the tool clamps and idler wheels.

thoughts on Dragon improving the breed:

• the debut of the Panzer IV series of super kits from Dragon is a real high point for the armor modeling hobby, especially German armor fans. Tamiya and Italeri had given us decent efforts, but barely good enough to make great models without a fair amount of extra detailing required. Today though, these Dragon kits are truly excellent models in that they are highly accurate and many of the details superbly molded and in-scale as much as plastic can be.

• Dragon's Panzer IV kits are also ever-evolving, so mistakes in one release are often corrected in the next version. While this is both good and bad, in the least we do end up with some very accurate kits for our choosing. This model was the original release #6264, but it remains the basic variant albiet all corrected and improved in the following Vorpanzer release, kit #6301, which I would then recommend for the basis of a similar DAK project as seen here.

tips for working with plastic parts to achieve superior scale thickness and add damage:

• I find it quite rewarding to utilize plastic parts whenever possible to showcase damage, whether it is dents and broken bits, or stuff that was shot up. The fenders on this kit are perfect candidates for this treatment due to the highly accurate detail that would take a lof of PE to replicate. So by using the kit fenders, I start by scraping a fresh hobby knife down the side of the fenders to thin them considerably. I then take small pliers and add dents and marks into the edges. For the front and rear fender flaps, I grind away as much plastic from the back sides as I can using a knife and grinding bit in my Dremel tool. I thin them to where I can actually see light through the plastic, and from there I can drill bullet holes or really bend them up as seen on the left rear fender.

PANZER IV AUSF E DAK

As nice as this Panzer IV kit is, construction is not a rapid endeavor, and overall it does require attention to detail due to the complex nature of the kit and the vageries present in the instructions, (a weak point of Dragon's kits), but it goes off mostly without a hitch and the complicated process of painting the model can finally begin.

BASE COLORS

Any time that you create a paintjob that is a result of two completely different camo schemes, such as the whitewash over the Dunkelgelb on the Panther, or the Sand on top of the Panzergrau done here, it is a benefit to the process to use a strong and non-lightened base camoflage. This is important because what transpires after you paint the second round of camo will literally destroy any efforts of lightening, fading, shading, even color modulation to a large degree. Thus, the effective solution to avoid this problem is to maintain a dark and strong base camo, so when the wear and tear does happen, that color underneath looks as it should.

• I had the process clear in my head how I wanted to paint this model. I knew with the sand camo being heavily distressed that my basecoat should visually be the basis to ensure I illustrate the chipping and paint wear and be recognizable as Panzergrau paint color underneath. Like the winter whitewash, once you spray the sand in rather opaque layers it will be impossible to shift the gray paint underneath afterwards.

• I also knew there would be a substantial amount of rubbing on this paint with the HS chipping, and later with the lacquer thinner removal technique, so I gave the basecoat one extra round of spraying to make certain I laid down enough paint to withstand the level of abuse I was about to impart upon it.

○ Stage One - primer layer via Mr. Surfacer 1200.

○ Stage Two - basecoat all of the exterior in the Panzergrau, and the interior for the chipping color under the Eifenbraun color.

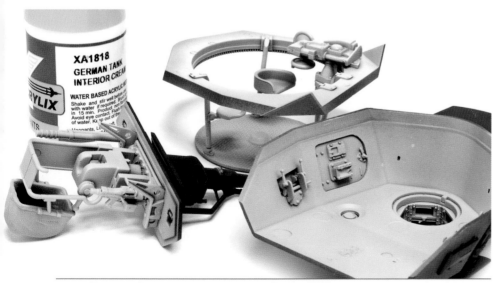

○ Stage Three - spray HS on the interior areas, then airbrush the Eifenbraun color over this, which will be chipped next.

With that concept in mind, I prime the entire model per my usual practice with Gunze's Mr. Surfacer 1200, and then go about painting the exterior in a strong Panzergrau color straight from the bottle using Lifecolor's dedicated Camouflage Series paint for this purpose, RAL 7021 Panzergrau. It has a fantastic hue that I imagine close to what a true Panzergrau should be with a hint of blue in it that we tend to prefer. Coverage is superb and it sprays beautifully thinned about 20% with water. These newer Lifecolor pre-packaged paint sets are of a thinner consistency than their UA line of paints and I've grown very fond of using them as often as possible.

TURRET NTERIOR
At this point, I now turn my attention to the interior of the turret. I wanted to add a myriad of chips and scratches that would be appropriate for a desert fighter and proceed to cover the turret assemblies in hairspray. I dry the HS and then paint the interior in Xtracrylix XA1818 German Tank Interior Cream for the standard issue Eifenbraun interior color. I had read good reviews on these paints and how they were very accurate out-of-the-bottle and I was quite happy using it. I was worried it looked too tan in the bottle, but once sprayed felt it had that just right look to iy.

I was also not too concerned with the fact the interior was already painted dark gray because once closed up, the details are very hard to see throught the small hatch openings and this model will eventually be displayed with figures in each hatch, further reducing the need to go

○ The turret interior chipped and ready for some weathering.

tips for chipping the turret interior:

• interiors that are largely closed up with only a few hatches to look through do not need to be given the full treatment, thus I concentrated on providing just enough wear and tear information to look believable to the viewer.

• the process itself is no different than any other HS chipping exercise, and I focused the efforts on anywhere the crew would likely have an adverse affect on the paint. That meant the hatch openings, and sills, the handles, the turret mechanisms and of course the treadplate floor received the most removal of the paint. I didn't bother with a red primer floor plate this time because it was almost impossible to see once the turret was closed up, it's so dark on the bottom of the hull.

• this was the first time that I had used an Xtracrylix paint color, and also the first time I had chipped their paint while using the HS technique. It performed flawlessly and the chips happened in much the same way as Lifecolor acrylic chips, which is generally quite good. Besides the short brush, I also used a toothpick to add in some sharp scratches and a bit more variety to the marks, all of which are going to get weathered next.

○ Chipping the interior with water and a short stiff bristled brush.

all out on painting accurate interior colors. I stuck mainly to the basics, and those areas that you would see close-up.

With water ready and my brushes in hand, I work the chipping around those interior areas the crew would likely do the most damage too, focusing on the hatch openings, the areas around them, where the crew would place their boots when entering and exiting the turret and so forth. I also chipped the gun breech and the control handles. It is all rather basic chipping, but would still be perfectly adequate once the turret was closed up. I wanted enough visual cues to illustrate my point, and didn't get too carried away.

But before I can close up the turret, I completed the weathering of said chipped areas by adding some simple washes and oil paint effectss to those same worn and affected areas to further distress and dirty the near-white paint. Grimy hands will cause this effect almost immediately as we can attest to in our daily lives, and the Germans certainly did not have ready access hand washing facilities nearby. Because I had kept the two side hatches movable, I spent extra time and effort with their inner faces since these will be the most visible on the final model in the open position. With that task finalized, I then paint the shell catch basket under the breech to wrap up the interior painting and weathering. I can

thoughts on weathering the interior areas:

• again this process is limited by its very nature of being hard to see, so I kept it simple and passable upon closer inspection. White interior paint is great to keep the tight space looking as spacious as possible, but it is also a magnet for dirty greasy hands, and that is exactly how I proceeded to treat the interior walls. I used Dark and Brown washes from MIG Prod. to highlight the details via pinwashes, and then used the 502 Abt. Shadow Brown oil paint to weather the chipped areas more.

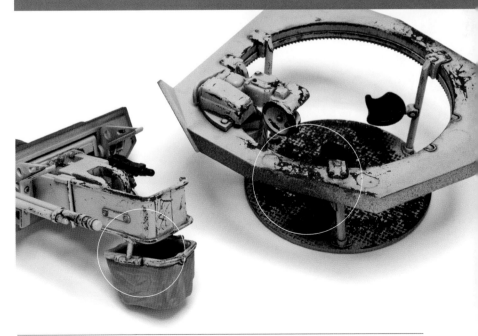

○ The finished turret interior areas are now ready to be closed up and remain largely hidden from view.

now close it up for good and prepare to get back onto the exterior painting.

As mentioned previously, once the turret is sealed at the front, there is prominent weld bead that must be added to the intricate joints common to this style of turret. I suppose I coul dof done all of the interior first, then painted the Panzergrau but I decided to only paint the color one time and be done with it, either way or process the results will be the same in the end. The reason is I used a simple weld bead technique of painting a thin line of Gunze's excellent Mr. Dissolved Putty around the glue joints, and after it dried for a fwe minutes added the weld texture with a modified toothpick, let that all dry for about 30 minutes, then simply handpainted the bead with a fine brush. Quite easy and no problems to report. Mr. Dissolved Putty is a great product to have handy for these sorts of odd needs.

WIth a fully assembled and painted model, I could now attend to the markings and painting the tools, spare tracks, exhausts and other exterior fittings not originally painted

○ The hatches were given extra weathering treatment due to the high traffic area and easy to see location.

○ **tips for working with Mr. Dissolved Putty and making weld beads:**

• there are definitely many ways to attack the issue of closing the turret, and I decided to do it this way to allow for easier interior painting and weathering. It was quite easy to deal with the weld bead after I had sealed the front up. Mr. Dissolved Putty is a great product for such tasks, and I work with it like a paint. I used a fine-tipped brush and carefully painted the bead onto the line I want to make the weld on, let it dry a few minutes and then I add the texture with a modified toothpick and a short jabbing motion as I move the toothpick along the weld line. The putty dries fast and is paintable, and the entire process only took a half hour or so.

thoughts on painting the tools and adding the markings:

• tool painting is sometimes more of a chore than anything else. On this project, I knew they were going to be oversprayed with the rest of the tank due to the hasty nature of the field applied camo. This is in contrast to the fact the original paint job is factory applied and the tools are not stored in their brackets during this process. In the early part of the war, the tools are issued to the unit after the tank is received by the company, so that means they should be painted in their natural state under the sand camo.

• I hand paint the tools using Lifecolor paints because they brush paint so well and cover the Lifecolor basecoat nicely. Sometimes switching paint brands can cause issues and I don't like painting with Vallejos unless I use a Vallejo basecoat for example. It's a minor preference, but one that works for me. And ultimately weathering any of these tools is minimal due to the heavy overspray involved later on.

• in any instance that I can use a spray mask or stencil to apply a marking I will, but the complicated crosses on the this model prevented me from using masks for those markings. The cross on the right side is actually applied in three elements over the antenna storage rack and hull side to look like a complete cross when from viewed in direct sideview elevation. Thus, the kit decals were used for this task, and I used metal DAK stencils from Voyager for the unique palm tree logos.

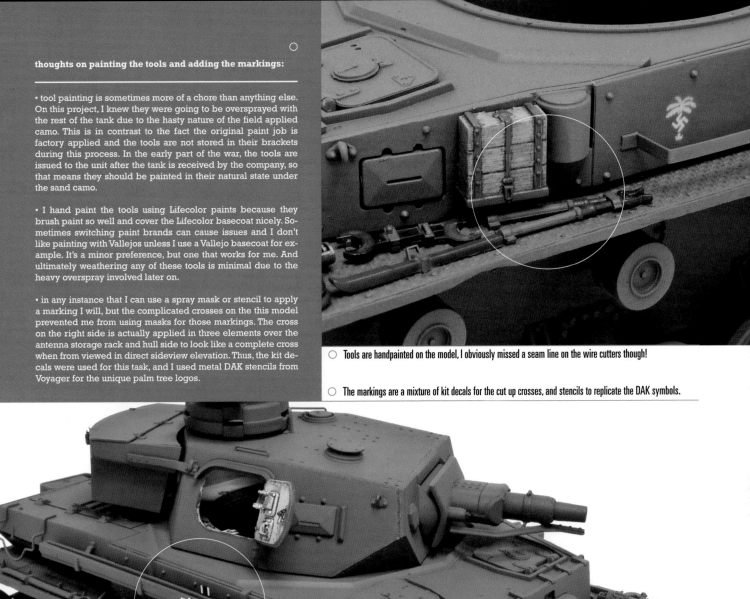

○ Tools are handpainted on the model, I obviously missed a seam line on the wire cutters though!

○ The markings are a mixture of kit decals for the cut up crosses, and stencils to replicate the DAK symbols.

173

in camoflage. At this period of the war, it was the factory process to paint the entire tank minus these parts, and then the crew would fit them once the tank arrived to the unit.

So I proceed to paint these items as appropriate with one exception. I incorrectly painted the fender mounted fire extinguisher in red, and it was later determined all exterior fire extinguishers are indeed supplied in base camo colors, which is either Panzergrau or Dunkelgelb. In my defence, it was always a contentious subject but evidence surfaced to make the case. But other than that, the colors of the fittings are accurate as shown in the photos. For wood tool handles, there is a range that would be acceptable, but my personal preference (for weathering purposes) is for a lighter hickory colored tool handle, but feel free to choose your wood color as needed.

As far as the markings go, I used a mix of decals from the kit for the side crosses in that unusual location across the hull side and the antenna mount, and then spray masks for the DAK symbol and secondary crosses on the hull. I liked the end result because it did give me a balance between a factory applied marking and the field applied palm tree DAK logos.

EXHAUST PAINTING

I'm nearly finsihed with the first level of painting, but I still had to attend to the exhaust muffler prominently displayed at the rear. By now, you are certain to realize I enjoyed myself with my favorite Lifecolor Rust paints. This time though, I did not want any original camo evident knowing I would have some heavily worn away sand camo applied later on. So I proceeded to paint the muffler in a more opqaue fashion the other exhausts in this book. I still use translucent layers and build up the colors slowly, but I arrive at a completely rust painted muffler in the end.

One additional step I do is to a final heavily faded tonal layer on top of this effect using

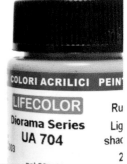
○ Stage One - the first layer of lightest rust is applied and completely covers the muffler.

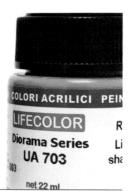
○ Stage Two - the next darker rust tone is applied in translucent layers as I build up the opacity.

○ Stage Three - moving to the base rust tone, the muffler is beginning to look like a properly rusted part.

○ Stage Four - the dark shadow rust color is applied in rather opaque layers and completely covers the entire muffler.

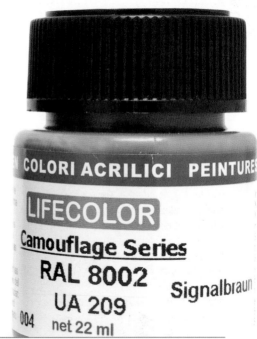

○ Stage Five - I used Signalbraun as a faded wash color and imparted a myriad of stains and moisture runoff effects with it.

thoughts on painting a desert tank exhaust: ○

• with the style of climate involved I wanted to give the exhaust system a different look than the other continetal based models in this book. With much less moisture available, I used colors that had a more faded look and less of the brighter oranges and yellow tones normally seen. I actually live in the desert and have come across a few abandoned mufflers during my hikes, and these tones are accurate to the drier setting. The muffler would undergo one more round of weathering after I paint the Sand camo and chip away most of the top paint to showcase the above painting, which as you may have guessed I really enjoyed doing.

• I could probably not explain this step enough. It is a question often asked when attempting to use hairspray. As described in the HS chapter, I hold the model at arms length and spray starting from the front of the model and stop after I pass the rear, much the same as is taught when using aerosol paints. You do not want to start spraying directly onto the model, instead start prior to it, move your hand across steady and quick, but not too fast, then end after you clear the rear. I rotate the model in my hand and ensure I cover every exposed area regardless if I will chip in those spots. It is far better to have HS in place and not needed then try to chip an area that did not get enough coverage, because it won't chip as you want and that's a frustrating episode.

• I use my hair dryer on low heat setting and completely dry off each layer. Then I proceed to spray the next one just as I did the first, and again I dry it off. Now the model is ready for the second round of painting and there is no need to wait any further amount of time.

The model resplendant in its base colors and painted details and entirely covered with two even layers of hairspray.

The camo painting begins on the lower hull to illustrate those areas that were not fully covered. The paint choices represent a field applied sand color first used by DAK forces.

○ With the lower hull sprayed, I then airbrush the rest of the model in a rather opaque fashion leaving key areas with slightly less sand paint as these will be the starting points for the chipping.

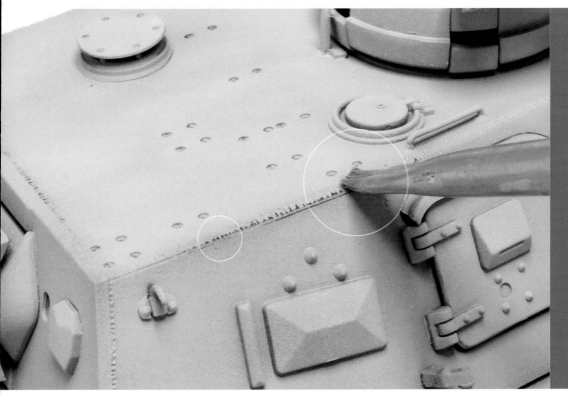

○

thoughts on the chipping:

• when I started the chipping process, I knew I wanted to make only the finest and most realistic marks that I could. To do this I learned to use not just the end of the bristles, but also the side of the brush itself to create really fine chips, especially along sharp edges such as shown to the left. By angling the brush slightly and using the side of the bristles, I move the brush side to side and this in effect rubs the paint off in a very controllable manner and I could make very fine chips as a result.

• chipping a large model such as this one takes time. In fact, it took nearly a week of evenings to see it completed and I would work on one section at a time, not rushing anything to ensure accuracy. I would often stop and study the wartime photos to see if there were some additional unique elements to the wear and tear and then try to add these to the model. I use some of my own creativity mixed with what I find during my research.

• going through the chipping and scratching stages, the model is really starting to come to life. It's exhilerating and pressure filled at the same time. Fortunately, the HS technique provides a level of control when you work slowly and with intent. Often times when the marks are being created, I start to get into a zone, a rhythm that really allows for me to get the most from the procedure. This is one of those enjoyable elements to the hobby where I am happiest at the bench, the model is becoming a reality and this spurns on even more motivation and ideas to create the best possible model that I can make.

• mistakes are also a part of the process. Every now and again the chips go astray and I stop immediately when I sense an area might have too much HS underneath (which can happen), and I try not to panic or get upset, even if it's a big mistake. I'll evaluate it and see if I can use the marks in the weathering somehow, or at worst attempt a spot respray to cover up the damage. Knowing how best to incorporate these issues makes for much less stress overall.

The results of the chipping on the rear exhaust, most of the sand being scrubbed away. I also carefully removed the sand camo from the cross and other battle damage.

The turret number is from the kit decal sheet and required lots of care and solvent to wrap around the details.

RAL 8002 Signalbraun color as a good choice to recreate this suitable effect. I really liked the end result because it stood out differently than my other efforts with these paints (I'm a big believer in not having identical looking models across my collection), and it fit the scenario of a dry climate rusted exhaust system.

HAIRSPRAY, THEN SAND CAMO

At this point in the painting, stage one is complete. The model is in its base Panzergrau camoflage, all the exterior fittings are painted and the markings are applied. Now comes the next and very critical stage of adding the hairspray layers, airbrushing the impromptu style sand camo and then distressing this paint layer in as accurate a process as I can muster.

To begin painting stage two, I spray the entire model in two even HS layers, drying off the first before spraying the second, which is then dried off again. Once dry, there is no need to wait further and I load the airbrush with a mixture of Lifecolor UA084 German Desert Yellow and UA090 Sand to represent the field applied color. I start by spraying the lower hull sides to replicate what I saw in my reference photos, it was a patchy hastily sprayed area and I wanted to capture the human element in this step. After that, I sprayed the rest of the model in a much stronger more opaque camo layer, and I used a trick to achieve a certain special effect while doing so. I first mounted the kit supplied tow cable, (which was

tips for working with the model's details to create the wear and tear in the paint: ○

• when I am chipping the paint, I try to always use the specifc area of the model to define where the marks will go. For example, the dents on the fender and heavily damaged areas are obvious spots to have more chips, and sharp edges too are commonly worn away spots. Raised details, and high use areas, such as the turret stowage bin get a lot of attention, as did the exhaust. I wanted to have most of the sand camo burned off by the high heat of the muffler, which provides a lot of visual contrast as well. Bullet holes and shrapnel damage too, each area was used as a starting point to chip that particular section, and in this manner I kept the paint wear and tear to a realistic level integrating the effects as I moved along.

○ The turret number decals were a challenge and I used Mr. Mark Softer to full affect, applying it multiple times to get the decals to stretch over the vision port, plus I had to slice them to fit tightly.

thoughts on paint wear via lacquer thinner:

• certanly one of the more unusual ideas I've used, the thought of rubbing off paint with thinner is risky to say the least. But it is also very realistic if done right and with care. The merits are valid for the specific sort of effect I was looking for.

• the type of brush is important and I found a worn #4 round tip brush very effective for the purpose. The worn ends of the bristles had just the right amount of friction to provide a soft worn effect. How much thinner was the most critical element and this required some practice to find the right level. Because of the power of the lacquer thinner, it was easy to rationalize that less is more, but in fact the brush must be nearly dry with only a hint of the thinner actually present on it. I kept a paper towel handy to constantly clean and re-wet the brush because the paint being worn off builds up in the bristles.

• once I found my sweet spot with this technique I was able to full intregrate the effects into the previous chipping efforts. And any spot that was worn too deep was simply touch upped afterwards. Sharp edges were usual suspects in that regards, but it proved an easy issue to deal with overall.

very nice by the way), to the rear hull mounting area to act as a spray mask. Photos showed it was often missing in the field showing the pattern created when the sand camo was obviously sprayed while it was still in place, and I wanted to show this off -- again all part of the story telling process. I also kept the turret stationary during this painting stage so that when it was later shown turned, it add even more emphasis that the sand was field applied.

CHIPS AND SCRATCHES

The next major step in the process was to chip and scratch the model with water and my favorite brushes and tools that I describe in the earlier HS chapter. In fact, I put a ton of focus on creating a lot of chips and scratches in-scale because I did not want the effect to overwhelm the model, yet still impart a clear visual impact that this tank has seen some action. These heavily worn effects are clearly seen in the many desert combat photos, so there is no de-

○ Work on the stowage bin emphasizes its constant use by the crew.

thoughts on paint wear on the upper turret:

• on the turret areas in particular, I combined the chipping and lacquer thinner removal process to impart a grittier worn paint effect as seen here. With the lacquer thinner brush in hand, I often held it at a very oblique angle to the surface, almost parallel sometimes to gently rub off the outer areas of the paint only with the sides of the bristles. A bit hard to describe, but it resembles dry-brushing motions in general. This method worked very well for the top plates of the turret and rear stowage bin, as shown at the left, as the gentle rubbing would very slowly begin to show the dark gray underneath. I could control this process to the maximum in this way and not have any major issues during.

• I was impressed with the realistic effects from this technique and like I said, it is naturally quite risky but at the same time can create very specific wear and tear, and thus it gets its turn on the technique round table in this project.

nying this fact, but I had to ensure they did not get too large and look unrealistic. This part is paramount and I can't emphasise this thought enough. The success of the model depended on me achieving this primary goal. So I start in one section and patiently, diligently work my way around imparting fina chips and scratches into the top layer of paint. The HS technique proving its worth with each stroke. However, my mind is processing an additional level of wear and tear and I had thoughts of doing this on the Tiger I to a certain extent, but here I had a mind to use it full effect.

LACQUER THINNER REMOVAL
I had a desire to try and replicate a worn off top layer of paint that was not necessarily chipped via the HS process. The sort of look one sees if you were to sand away the top coat intentally but I couldnit use sand paper or steel wool because I needed much greater control and be able to get into all the tight spaces for a realistic look. I also wanted to compliment the chipping and work with for an overall cohesive finish.

To acheive this deisred effect, I decided to experiment and use some paint thinner on a brush and rub the top layer of paint to see what results I could get. So I set up a scrap model section painted in the same two colors and began to practice. After a few tries at the idea, I

○ The upper main gun is also a common area of crew movement for maintenance purposes, plus its regular use from firing.

○ The rear hull plate saw extensive damage and was given extra efforts to portay this effectively.

thoughts on additional paint wear via lacquer thinner:

• this process could also be used for more deliberate effects such as further chipping and harsher looking wear and tear around the hatch openings and along the sharper edges of the armor. This was achieved by simply swapping to a small firmer brush that could create smaller areas of paint wear.

• the main idea here being this process would bridge the visual and physical differences between the HS chipping, and the previous softer smoother looking lacquer thinner removal areas. In this manner I could have a rather seamless, yet extreme, level of outer paint wear and attend to each section in its own unique way. The combination of these two effects plays into my overriding themes of layering processes and trying to maintain all of the weathering in-scale. And I must reinforce the notion of practicing such ideas on scrap models prior to actually attempting them on your final model.

realized it started to work quite well when the brush had almost no thinner on it. By carefully scrubbing away at the paint I could (after some time) remove it in a much softer looking style than the sharper looking chips and scratches. This was exactly the effect I had in mind, so I prepared myself to attack the model with the lacquer thinner as I had just practiced. It was a bit nerve wracking to say the least and it is a delicate thing to do, so I highly recommend you proceed in a similar fashion and practice this before attempting it on the real model. There were also a few spots I overworked and I did have to go back retouch some edge in the base colors again, but overall the technique worked as I had hoped. I focused my efforts along all of the top surfaces, basically anywhere the crew would work, sit and move around. And I could also impart some sharper edged areas by using a smaller brush as shown below, and by using this method along with the HS chipping I was able to fully realize the extensive level of paint wear that I had seen in the reference photos.

○

thoughts on the model to this stage and preparing for the next weathering stages:

• At this point the model is heavily weathered to look like a true veteran combatant. Comparing the visual effects to those seen in some of the more extreme wartime photos keeps the process moving and on track. I had certain goals to illustrate the very unique nature of this field applied camo scheme that was very temporary at best.

• from here the next weathering phases will start to add color back into the model and build up the depth to each area that really makes the model successful. I am already thinking in my head at this point what colors I want to use for the pinwashes and filters, I'm thinking about the range of tones and what would work and what wouldn't. I'm also studying my paint wear and seeing where I could add oils to render other effects like streaks and staining so when I come back over those areas again, I have a good plan of action.

○ The end results of both the HS chipping and the lacquer thinner removal technique. The combination of fine chips and scratches is blended in with the softer worn away areas.

○ In every section of the model the worn areas are dictated by what's there, whether it be a tool, spare tracks, or damage to the surface of the tank.

tips for achieving success with the worn paint effects:

• there is a constant challenge to replicate each special effect in-scale and this takes practice, the right tools and patience to not rush through them too quickly. I work with one section at a time, get most of it done, move to the next one until I have the entire model completed, then I go back and begin to work certain spots again that may need more attention, slowly building up each area until I'm happy with it. Again, I am constantly checking back to my references to ensure I don't get too carried away or stray too far out of scale. And always take a moment to step back and evaluate the progress.

thoughts on using filters and pinwashes on a desert tank:

• the dry arid desert climate creates a totally different set of weathering parameters than a moist climate. There is far less build up of dirt and grime around small details because the desert dust has far less sticking power in its dry state. Plus deserts tend to be high wind areas, acting much the same as open oceans in how they heat and cool the air creating wind in the process, which of course blows the dry dust off and around constantly. So we must take this into account.

• for the pinwash, a slightly darker color to the base tone is preferrable and then it is applied very sparingly to the details. Nothing too intense, just enough of an effect to bring out some of the details, but the contrast should remain quite low.

• for the filters, the light sand camo can react very quickly to any shift in tones and therefore I decided to basically spot filter specific panels and hatches to break up the sand color in a much more subtle manner. Using filters in this way makes a lot of sense because the tint builds up very slowly so there is maximum control over the process. I only wanted a very mild tonal shift, nothing dramatic.

tips for combining multiple methods to arrive at the end result:

• because I was not applying pigments in my usual thicker manner and was really focusing on utilizing a very thin layer of dust, I could incorporate other processes to affect the overall color balance and weathering that I would not normally get to do. Because there was still a lot of visible paint areas under the dust pigments, I could alter the tones of these areas with both filters and pinwashes together. I was able to add streaks and other stains all in an effort to increase the visual interest down on the lower hull.

• In this same manner, I used the filters, pinwashes and the pigments on the upper hull areas to achieve the dry desert climate look I was after. Strong moisture stains were kept to a minimum and I focused more on subtle detail enhancements that helped to draw the viewer in closer. The camera is great at capturing them as seen at left and below, but once you stand back and see the overall results they are quite subtle and work to blend in naturally with the previous processes.

A combination of pigments and filters create subtle color shifts on the lower hull areas and hatches.

PINWASH, FILTERS, AND PIGMENTS

This model stood in stark contrast to any of my previous efforts, the desert scheme are definitely unique and require so focus to ensure they maintain that look all the way through to the end. After the extended time spent chipping and wearing away the paint with the thinner, I could now push onwards and the next level of weathering. Next, I add a pinwash and filter layer, however on this project I wanted a distinctly different look. Studying desert photos I realized the pinwash should be very mellow in tone and just give the slightest hint of shadow, too dark and it would immediately look more like a tank from the continent, and not fighting in the dry desert theater. Same with the filter, almost any color would richen the sand too much so instead of one overall filter, I decided to only filter certain panels, to break up the surface a little bit more. This worked quite well in the end and I was able to give the model some needed depth and still keep the desert theme strongly intact.

Same goes for the pigments, I knew I couldn't simple layer them on as I usually do, but I certainly wanted to add some simple dust colors that would still look like desert dust on top the light sand camo. This was a bit trickier than it looked and I worked in only the lightest

• there are a couple of methods of applying pigments to recreate thin dusty layers on the model and for this project I used one I like a lot and get tons of use from. It starts with mixing up the right color batch, and I wanted the color slightly lighter than the sand camo so it would be visible and not make the model any darker. With that ready, I use a brush and apply small amounts directly to the surface where I want it and then scrub it in a natural manner. As I descibe in previous chapters, I then load some fixer into my airbrush (I used Tamiya X-20A thinner here), and gently mist it onto the area from around 6 inches away letting it gently fall onto the surface wetting the pigments as it hits. It dries almost instantly and sets the pigments in place, just enough so I can work in additional effects.

The pre-assembled track runs are sprayed in a basecoat mixture of Tamiya paints shown above.

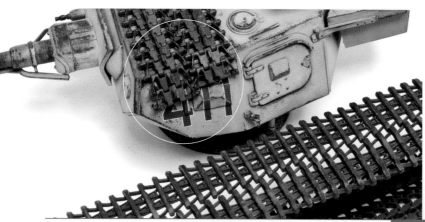

Test fitting the spare tracks to seee how they look against the model's tones.

Close up of the painted tracks with its subtle textures, they are ready for some pigments now.

pigment colors I had. One aspect of the pigments is that they are so matte it really added a subtle visual transition element from painted metal to the dustier sections. For the application itself, I wanted to avoid tide marks at all costs, so I used the same airbrush method to spray on the fixer in light mist layers to set the pigments in place once I dusted a section. I worked the pigments into the model until I was happy with the dusty appearance.

TRACKS

Provided in the kit are some impressive link-to-link 40cm wide tracks that come in bags already removed from their sprues. Plus they are handed and cast in slightly different color grays to help us keep them sorted properly. To assemble them, I first lay down on my bench a strip of 1/4" wide double stick tape approximately the length of each track run, and then simply click the links of each run together on top of the tape, which is conventiently holding them in place for me. The links click together well enough, but they are not workable systems and will fall apart right away, so the tape is like the third hand. I then add a drop of Tamiya Extra Thin Cement between each link and this sets up to dry for about 15 minutes. That may seem long, but the joints are just plyable and strong enough to remove each run from the tape, wrap it around the road wheels, secure it with a piece of tape and add some accurate track sag. I do this process twice obviously, then set the model aside to let the tracks dry completely overnight. I am careful to not glue the tracks to

thoughts on painting and weathering the tracks:

• like exhausts, tracks are usually going to be finished is some shade of earth and rust tones. While not a hard and fast rule, it is a relevant color spectrum to work within on most projects. I prefer to start with a tone that will represent the theater of action best, and I wanted a brown shade with a hint of rust and gray to it, in an effort to illustrate a tank operating in a barren landscape. I wasn't going to benefit heavily from adding lots of dirt and earth tones because of the dry terrain prevented such circumstances, so I kept the pigments to a minimum in the end.

• I also decided against adding bright worn areas on these tracks because the model was already at a point of showcasing a lot of visual effects both strong and subtle, and showing bright freshly worn tracks was too much in my opinion here. So I went the other direction and kept them in a rusted state indicative of a tank that had not moved recently, or at least for a few days. All possible given down time for maintenance and calm periods between troop movements and combat action, and part of my efforts to tell the story of this tank and why and how it came to be presented in the state I am showing it in.

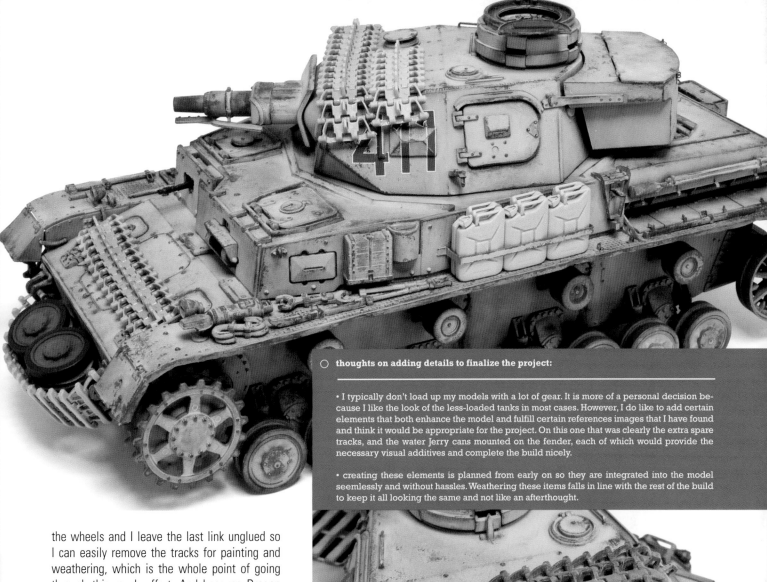

○ thoughts on adding details to finalize the project:

• I typically don't load up my models with a lot of gear. It is more of a personal decision because I like the look of the less-loaded tanks in most cases. However, I do like to add certain elements that both enhance the model and fulfill certain references images that I have found and think it would be appropriate for the project. On this one that was clearly the extra spare tracks, and the water Jerry cans mounted on the fender, each of which would provide the necessary visual additives and complete the build nicely.

• creating these elements is planned from early on so they are integrated into the model seemlessly and without hassles. Weathering these items falls in line with the rest of the build to keep it all looking the same and not like an afterthought.

the wheels and I leave the last link unglued so I can easily remove the tracks for painting and weathering, which is the whole point of going through this much effort. And because Dragon provides us with plenty of extra links, I create five additional spare track armor sections that I will use to cover the front of the hull with and place on top of the turret, as was often in done by the DAK armor units.

After these were all dry and solid, I removed the tracks and prime them accordingly. To paint them I used a blend of Tamiya acrylics to create a dark grayish-red brown base color from *XF-69 NATO Black* and *XF-79 Linoleum Deck Brown*, which I then airbrush on. Next I mix some rust colored washed together and apply these with a sponge all along each main run and spare track section to create a subtle dried rust tone. However, I think

○ The completed spare tracks in place on the turret roof, a common sight with DAK units.

PANZER IV AUSF E DAK

○ Stage Three - begin to use mapping in the white to further add depth, and add rust with OPR.

○

thoughts on the final details of the project:

• details, details, details -- the thought process never ends and this includes accessories and stowed items, as well as the painting and weathering elements. This model has a tremendous level of fine details built into the finish, and many are not seen from a distance until you are up close to the surface will these efforts becomes clear. This was part of my original goal to showcase this concept that is part of what we see in the reference photos. All the while luring the viewer in closer and then rewarding them with more visual data. It is by using methods like the HS technique and the lacquer thinner removal idea that are capable of achieving these targets, and by realizing my end result, I worked backwards to decide on what would be the best path to follow in order to get there successfully.

○ The combination of the HS chipping, lacquer thinner removal worked together to achieve the worn paint effects.

○ The ever important spare water cans are always clearly marked with white crosses to avoid confusion with fuel cans.

the effects were too subtle and are hardly noticeable in the end, but I still felt they looked like proper desert tracks in the end.

I finish them off with the same pigments that I used on the model, applying them dry first, then adding the fixer, this time with a brush so they flow more into the myriad of holes and details on the links. I can then put the tracks back on the model and glue the final link together to hold them firmly in place. Afterwards, I was happy that they looked liked they were not used often because I wanted to avoid the cliche look of having bright metal cleats showing. Often in the desert campaign there was a lot of downtime for these tanks with the lulls between fighting, so it wouldn't be out of place to have all the exposed track surfaces rusted over after sitting for a few days.

The next to last order of business was to get the spare road wheels in place and weather them to match the rest of the model. For a splash more color I painted the road wheel mounted on the right hand side of the hull in primer red, and placed the gray ones on the nose, supported by the spare tracks mounted there, which I then add pigments to. The last bit of painting was for the water cans mounted on the left fender. I painted them in the same order as the tank -- Panzergrau first, HS layer, then the sand camo that was chipped and worn away. The white crosses are sprayed via dedicated masks by Eduard for German Jerry cans, and I added slightly darker filters to the three of them to help visually set them off from the tank better.

193

Sd.Kfz 161

The workhorse of the German armor corps has been faithfully reproduced by Dragon in a fantastic 1/35 series of Panzer IV kits, starting off with this 3-in-1 release, which was used to represent a DAK unit in all its wornout glory. So much effort was put into the project to arrive at the completed stage with a convincing model that exhibits a strong number of weathering effects. The challenge of the desert is never-ending for us as modelers in our efforts to capture the look and feeling that goes along with this very specifc region of combat.

The challenge is then set forth to arrive at the end in a succesful manner that represents an honest model true to the conditions of the events that took place. It starts with the history of the first DAK units to arrive in their dark gray camo and requiring immediate desert camo paint to make these near black vehicles blend into the light sand terrain. And from this story, how the uints were pressed into action at Tobruk and the effects of the harsh landscape and combat action would leave the tanks looking battered at best. What a challenge it is to be able to sit down with a great kit, all the while having inspirational reference at hand to lay the foundations of this project. Couple these elements with some amazing painting and weathering techniques and the recipe was cast for a project that would provide a true modeling experience from start to finish.

PANZERKAMPFWA

Pz Kpfw IV Ausf E DAK mit 7.5cm KwK37 L/24

GEN IV AUSF E DAK

PRIMER

BASE COAT

INTERIOR OVER HAIRSPRAY LAYER

CHIPPING W/WATER

PINWASHES

INTERIOR HATCH WEAR

NEW WELD BEADS

FINAL CAMO

MARKINGS & DETAIL PAINTING

EXHAUST PAINTING

HAIRSPRAY LAYER

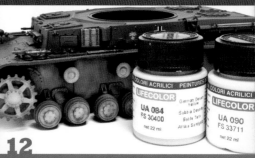

DESERT CAMO

QUICK REF SBS

FINAL MARKINGS

TURRET CHIPPING & WEAR

HEAVY CHIPPING

LACQUER THINNER REMOVAL

LACQUER THINNER CHIPPING

ENGINE DECK WEAR

LIGHT BWN PINWASH

FILTER PANELS

LOWER HULL WEATHERING

PIGMENTS

TRACKS & SPARE TRACK ARMOR

FINAL DETAILS & STOWAGE

FIGURE MODELING

models, photos and text by Marijn van Gils

Many articles and books have described how to paint figures: colors, techniques of application, etc. But rarely you can read about and see exactly where the different colors are being applied. Therefore, I would like to focus this chapter on explaining where to paint what. Hopefully this will provide you with a better understanding of where to place highlights, shadows, etc. and why.

CONTRAST AND HARMONY

When painting figures, most time is devoted to carefully highlighting and shading every part of them. There is a very good reason for this: it is the main way of instilling life into the subject. By painting shadows and highlights on every single element of our project, we emphasize the three-dimensionality of it. This is necessary because light doesn't behave the same on a 1/35 version as on the real thing. We need to bring a lot of extra contrast into our models to make them feel much larger, heavier, and more detailed than they actually are. It is, however, crucial not to let this contrast affect the harmony of the model. For example, exaggerated shadows can make a figure look over the top and unharmonious, and therefore unrealistic. So, the key question is: how can we combine maximum contrast (which brings life) and harmony (a natural look) into our figures?

OVERHEAD LIGHTING

The answer is a correct and precise placement of highlights and shadows. The best place to paint them is exactly where the light naturally falls on the figure. If we simply emphasize the natural shadows instead of creating conflicting ones, the result will look much more natural. Moreover, it will make it possible to get much more contrast. For example, if we paint shadows where they naturally don't fall precisely, they will quickly look overdone and we will stop darkening them (and thus adding contrast) quickly. On the other hand, if we paint the shadows following the natural shadows, we can go as dark as we want, often even ending with pure black for the deepest ones, achieving thereby maximum contrast and maximum life.

A Hurried Descent
British balloon observers take their chance on the first operational parachutes when under aircraft attack during WWI (2005, 1/35).

It is a widespread misconception that you can put too much contrast in a paintjob. This is not true: the more contrast the better! But you can create inappropriate contrast by painting shadows and highlights in the wrong places. This will in the beginning certainly happen to you due to lack of technical control and finesse of handling the brush. Don't worry, you will learn this with time and practice. The second reason for misplacing shadows and highlights is much more important: a lack of knowledge and feeling of where to put them.

Don't worry, this is also something which can be learned, and this article/chapter is meant to help you with it. Maybe it might be a comforting thought that almost every figure painter constantly works on improving these skills further? Therefore, perfection is not expected; slowly trying to get closer to it one project at a time is all we can do.

So, where do these natural shadows and highlights fall? This depends of course on the light source(s) present, which means that our painted shadows and highlights will never be perfect for every viewing situation. So it is best to choose the most common light source in which our figure is most likely to be viewed. Undoubtedly, in most cases this light will come from directly above. This is the exact meaning of the often used terms "overhead lighting" and "zenithal lighting": painting with the light coming from above.

IN PRACTICE

As every figure is different, every figure needs a slightly different placement of highlights and shadows, but that's the fun of it. There is however a simple trick to know where to paint shadows and highlights: hold the figure under a bright lamp and study the light. Where the surface is lighted by the lamp: paint highlights. Where you see shadows: paint shadows. Simple, no?

Note how not only the details are painted according to overhead lighting, like for example the fingers on his left hand, but also the main volumes. The shoulder is lighter than the chest, and the upward facing part of the arms are lighter than their lower half.

Survival of The Fittest: French brothers in arms fight over the last working gas mask at the onset of a gas attack during WWI (2005; 1/35).

FIGURE MODELING

Of course, there is a lot to be seen on the surface of a figure, and achieving top results is really in the details. Therefore, it is a good idea to actively study the figures of top painters, photographs of real people and portrait paintings, and of course to practice a lot. This will develop your ability to analise a figure enormously.

Mistakes are of course ok, as we can learn a lot from them, especially about what not to do. A common figure-painting mistake is to highlight protruding elements completely, not just the parts of them that actually catch light. Usually this is combined with shading the entire deeper lying areas, not only the part that are actually in shadow. Instead, we really need to observe where the light is falling, and not just assume it. For example on vertical surfaces of clo-

thing, the top of protruding parts will be light (the lower part of horizontal folds), but the underside will be dark (the upper part of folds). The transition between light and dark will actually take place on the tip of the protruding part.

Another common mistake is to forget the that details are part of a larger volume. Many people fall in the trap of highlighting and shading every single fold to the maximum, forgetting that they are part of an entire garment. But of course a fold on the underside of a sleeve will have less light and more shadow than a fold on the top of the same sleeve. It is thus important not to bring out only the three-dimensionality of details, but the three-dimensionality of the entire figure. Don't only focus on highlighting and shading the folds, but make sure that the entire volume is shaded and highlighted: shoulders lighter, vertical surfaces a bit less light, undersides of arms dark, etc.

201

Santa is coming to town! (2004; 1/35). In AFV dioramas, figures are often the protagonists. Therefore, they deserve all the time and effort you put in them.

THE STEP-BY-STEPS

The step-by-steps show how I usually paint the mayor elements of a figure: a face and some simple pieces of clothing. I provided the Humbrol colors I used to give you an idea, but I would only advise Humbrol enamels to modelers who are already very experienced with them. For anyone else, I feel acrylics are far easier to get good results, unless of course you prefer artists oils. No paint medium is better than the other; and it is possible to get top level results with any of them. My color mixes might also be overly complex for most people, so don't pay too much attention to those. The exact colors to use is very much a matter of taste, style, and the effect you are looking for (a tanned soldier in the desert or a freezing figure in the Russian winter), so I would encourage you to experiment freely.

Each step-by-steps is subdivided in several sessions. I usually execute these on different days for the paint to dry between each session. This of course not necessary if you work with acrylics. I included the time I need for each session, just to give you an idea of the time

Step-by-step: faces (paint numbers are for Humbrol)

• Session 1: Base (2 x 5min of work)
A good solid basecoat is important. I applied two thin layers of flesh 61+ wine 73 + natural wood 110 + a bit of blue 104 (to desaturate the color a bit). Let this dry overnight when using enamels, if you don't want them to dissolve during the highlighting session.

• Session 2: Highlighting (1h 30min of work)
First highlight - Highlighting is done very slowly in number of layers to obtain smooth transitions. As I like to start with a rather dark base, I need quite a lot of layers. You can start much lighter, but this will require more work when shading. Just a matter of preference. If you work with Humbrol, it is best to apply another coat of the base color before the first highlight so you can blend these together at the transition. With acrylics, this is not necessary.

Second highlight - Note how small the differences are between the base, the first highlight and the second highlight. If you want soft transitions of the highlights, it is best to build up the effect gradually. To highlight, I simply add more flesh 61 to the base color. When this becomes as light as pure flesh 61, I replace it by pure flesh 61 and add some white 34. But we are not there yet.

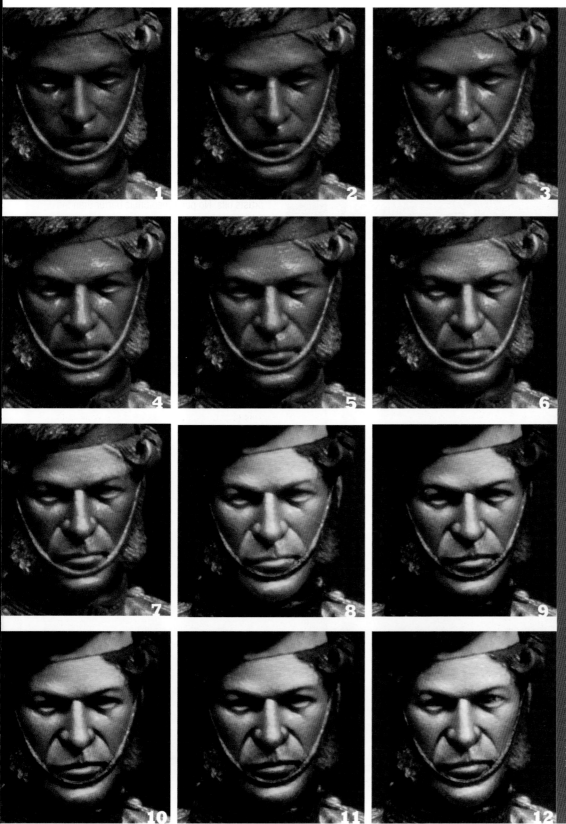

Third highlight - Slowly, it becomes more apparent where the highlights are being placed:
- forehead
- upper eyelids
- upper edge (not the front!) of the lower eyelids
- bridge of the nose
- top of the nostrils
- on and above the cheekbones (gradually lightening towards the lower eyelids)
- zone between nose and mouth (gradually lightening towards the folds between the corners of the mouth and the nose, at the same time lightening upwards, and finally adding a subtle thin highlight directly above the upper lip)
- top of the lower lip
- top, as in upper part, of the chin (again not the front!)

Fourth highlight - Gradually building up the effect will avoid most harsh transitions, but after every coat, small corrections are made to the transitions if necessary. With Humbrol, this is done by blending the edge of the two colors gently with a fine brush moistened with White Spirit. With acrylic paint, the hard edge is overpainted with an intermediate color.

Fifth highlight - From this step on, I used only pure flesh 61 + white 34. Note how the lighter areas gradually reduce in size. On the forehead, for example, only to top area and the top of the eyebrows are highlighted any further.

Sixth highlight - This last step, using a very light color with more white 34 than flesh 61, adds a lot of contrast and life, even though only tiny areas are painted with it.

Correction of the highlighting - This step is usually not needed. Unfortunately, I kept the highlighted areas rather small, causing the overall flesh-tones to look too dark and the contrast to feel too unnatural for my taste. This is of course, purely a matter of style and taste. Many painters might actually prefer the look of the previous photo. The solution was simple however: using the different highlight colors, I expanded the highlighted areas until I was happy. This causes the face to look lighter overall. Painting is always a bit of messing about! Luckily, otherwise it would merely be painting by numbers.

• Session 3: Shading (1hr of work)

First shadow - Wine 73 + black 33 + a bit of natural wood 110 (to desaturate the colour a bit), strongly diluted and applied:
- on the eyeballs (as shadow under the upper eyelids and as base for the eyes)
- under the brows (darkest towards the nose)
- underside of the lower eyelids (darker towards the nose)
- under the nose
- in the folds between the corners of the mouth and the nose (darkest towards the nose)
- on the entire upper lip
- under the lower lip (darkest in the middle, and usually no shadow towards the sides)
- under the entire chin and jaw
Multiple transparent coats of the same diluted colour are used to obtain gradually darker shadows.

Second shadow - Only wine 73 + black 33, which is almost black, again strongly diluted, applied only on the darkest spots. Finally, I apply some pure black 33 on the eyeballs, and usually also in the corner of the brows and nose, under the nose (at the nostrils), in the deepest part of the ears, and at the darkest point under the lower lip.

• Session 4: finishing (30min to 1hr of work, depending on how lucky I get with the eyes)
This session can immediately follow the shading session, but with enamels it is easier to make any corrections without spoiling previous work if the shadows have dried overnight.

Color - With strongly diluted wine 73 (a bordeaux-red), some colour is added to:
- the cheeks
- lower sides of the nose
- earlobes
- lower lip
Be careful to keep this subtle, and refrain from painting the lower lip a bright red. You wouldn't want your military figure to appear to wear lipstick! The five o'clock shadow is painted on with strongly diluted black 33. Be careful not to touch the highest highlights on the top of the chin and directly above the upper lip, so they retain their effect. The addition of the warm red and the cold grey (black) cause a nice contrast in colour which adds a lot of variation and life to the face.

Eyes - The white of the eyes consists of white 34 + natural wood 110. As this figure looks sideways (which usually adds more life to the face and is easier to paint), I only applied it to one corner of the eyes, leaving the rest black. A 'reflection' in the form of a small dot of light blue (blue 104 + white 34) brings the eye alive. It is critical to get the eyes symmetric, both in shape, size and position of the iris and reflection. This often demands a lot of messing around, retouching, and more retouching, often including retouches to the eyelids. Patience is key.

Finally, satin varnish is added to (and only to) the highlighted areas of the face. This mimics the smoother texture and slight shine of real skin. A face always looks better when the surrounding hairs and clothes have been painted with the same care.

The finished figure as part of the tiny diorama *Van Gils Construction* (2008; 54mm and 1/700).

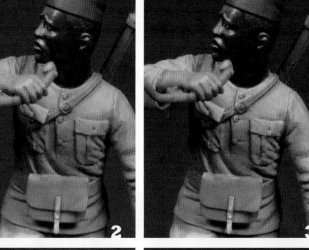

Part 1: jacket
• Session 1: Base (2 x 5min of work)

The base-coat is mixed from desert yellow 93, natural wood 110 and black 33, applied in two thin coats and left to fully harden.

• Session 2: Highlighting (1hr 30min of work)

After the same color is applied again and left to dry for a couple of minutes (only necessary when working with enamels), the first highlight is applied. Note how little difference can be seen with the previous image.

Second Highlight - With every highlight, some more desert yellow is mixed with the base color.

Third Highlight - From this step on, I also added some radome tan 148 to the mix.

Fourth highlight - It is becoming apparent where the highlights are placed. Most folds receive highlights, but the upward facing surfaces of the arms and shoulders are the lightest. The entire volume is highlighted, not only the individual folds.

Fifth and last highlight - Pure radome tan 148 was painted to very restricted areas: the edge of the collar, the seam of the left arm, and the upper edges of the chest pockets. Note how throughout highlighting, folds are divided in an upper area which is left dark, and a lower area which is highlighted. Note also that not all folds are highlighted equally intensively. Folds on the upper surfaces are highlighted much further than folds on the downward facing surfaces.

• Session 3: Details (1h of work)

Details like the red piping, the belt, ammunition pouch and gun-strap receive their base-coats. I find it easier to do this after highlighting the main parts of the shirt, so I don't have to be too careful when highlighting the main surfaces.

Every detail gets highlighted individually. Note how it is really only the upper edge of the strap and belt that receive the main highlights. The piping stitched-on effect is painted in *trompe l'oeil*, for which it's upper surfaces receive a clear highlight. If there would be any glossy spots after this stage hardens, I would now apply a layer of matt varnish.

• Session 4: Shading (1h of work)

9. First, the extreme shadows are applied with diluted black 33. On almost anything

205

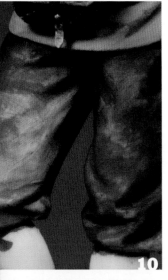

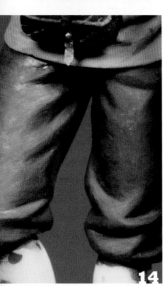
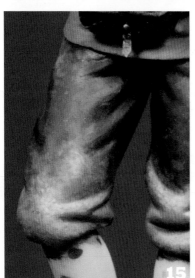
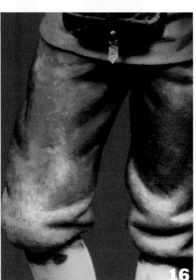
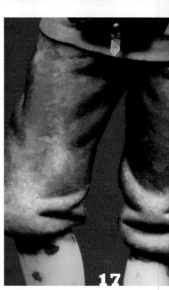

The finished figure: *I want to ride my bicycle!*

A Belgian-Congolese bicycle trooper struggling with the difficult terrain of East-Africa during WW1 (2006; 1/35)

you should expect to invest for this level of results. Of course, some people need more and some need less for the same result. It is certainly possible to paint much faster than this (which can be a good idea if you need to paint 50 figures for a massive diorama, or if you are not the most patient person or simply don't want to spend more time on it, which is all perfectly fine), but this will of course decrease the finesse of your work. You can only get out of a figure what you put into it.

A high level of finesse can only be achieved through years of practice, so please don't get discouraged if your first (or even 30th) figure doesn't look exactly like the ones in this chapter. Don't expect perfect results immediately, just enjoy the process of slowly building up your level of finesse and seeing every figure get a bit better than the previous one.